GODWIN ON WOL

CLASSIC BIOGRAPHIES
EDITED BY RICHARD HOLMES

Defoe on Sheppard and Wild
Johnson on Savage
Godwin on Wollstonecraft
Southey on Nelson
Gilchrist on Blake
Scott on Zélide

GODWIN ON WOLLSTONECRAFT

Memoirs of the Author of
'The Rights of Woman'

by
William Godwin

EDITED WITH AN INTRODUCTION BY
RICHARD HOLMES

HARPER PERENNIAL
London, New York, Toronto and Sydney

Harper Perennial
An imprint of HarperCollins*Publishers*
77–85 Fulham Palace Road,
Hammersmith, London w6 8jb

www.harperperennial.co.uk

This Harper Perennial Classic Biography published 2005
1

Memoirs of the Author of 'The Rights of Woman' first published 1798

Introduction Copyright © Richard Holmes 2005

A catalogue record for this book is
available from the British Library

ISBN 0-00-711176-2

Set in PostScript Linotype Adobe Caslon
and Spectrum Display by
Rowland Phototypesetting Ltd,
Bury St Edmunds, Suffolk

Printed and bound in Great Britain by
Clays Ltd, St Ives plc

CONTENTS

INTRODUCTION

1

It is often said that William Godwin's *Memoirs of the Author of 'The Rights of Woman'* of 1798 destroyed Mary Wollstonecraft's reputation for over 100 years. If that is true, it must count as one of the most dramatic, as well as the most damaging, works of biography ever published.

At the time of her death in London on 10 September 1797, Mary Wollstonecraft was certainly well-known and widely admired, as an educational writer and champion of women's rights. She was renowned not only in Britain, but also in France, Germany and Scandinavia (where her books had been translated), and in newly-independent America. Although only 38 years old, she was already one of the literary celebrities of her generation.

The *Gentleman's Magazine*, a solid large-circulation journal of record with a conservative political outlook, printed the following obituary in October 1797, with an admiring – if guarded – summary of her career and an unreservedly favourable estimate of her character.

> In childbed, Mrs Godwin, wife of Mr. William Godwin of Somers-town; a woman of uncommon talents and considerable

knowledge, and well-known throughout Europe by her literary works, under her original   name of Wollstonecraft, and particularly by her *Vindication of the Rights of Woman*, 1792, octavo.

Her first publication was *Thoughts on the Education of Daughters*, 1787 . . . her second, *The Rights of Man*, 1791, against Mr Burke on the French Revolution, of the rise and progress of which she gave an *Historical and Moral View*, in 1794 . . . her third, *Elements of Morality for the Use of Children, Translated from the German*, 1791 . . . her fourth, *A Vindication of the Rights of Woman*, 1792 . . . her fifth, *Letters Written during a Short Residence in Sweden, Norway and Denmark*, 1796.

Her manners were gentle, easy and elegant; her conversation intelligent and amusing, without the least trait of literary pride; or the apparent consciousness of powers above the level of her sex; and for soundness of understanding, and sensibility of heart, she was perhaps, never equaled. Her practical skill in education was even superior to her speculations upon that subject; nor is it possible to express the misfortune sustained, in that respect, by her children. This tribute we readily pay to her character, however adverse we may be to the system she supported in politicks and morals, both by her writing and practice.

Many other favourable articles appeared, such as her friend Mary Hays's combative obituary in the *Monthly Magazine* for September 1797, which lauded her 'ardent, ingenuous and unconquerable spirits', and lamenting that she was 'a victim to the vices and prejudices of mankind'. The *Monthly Mirror* praised her as 'a champion of her sex', and promised an imminent biography, though this did not appear. Friends in London, Liverpool, Paris, Hamburg, Christiana, and New York expressed their shock at her sudden departure, one of the earliest, premature Romantic deaths of her generation. It seemed doubly ironic that the champion of women's rights should have died in childbirth.

William Godwin, her husband, was devastated. They had been lovers for little over a year, and married for only six months. At 42 he also was a literary celebrity, but of a different kind from Mary. A shy, modest and intensely intellectual man, he was known paradoxically as a firebrand philosopher: the dangerous radical author of *An Enquiry Concerning Political Justice* (1793) and the political thriller-novel *Caleb Williams* (1794). His views were even more revolutionary than hers. He proposed republican, atheist and anarchist ideas, attacking many established institutions, such as private property, the Church, the monarchy, and (ironically) marriage itself – 'that most odious of monopolies'. Indeed he was notorious for his defence of 'free love', and their marriage in March 1797 had been the cause of much amusement in the press. Yet Godwin believed passionately in the rational power of truth, and the value of absolute frankness and sincerity in human dealings.

He was in a state of profound shock. He wrote bleakly to his oldest friend and confidante, the playwright Thomas Holcroft on 10th September 1797, the very evening of her death: 'My wife is now dead. She died this morning at eight o'clock . . . I firmly believe that there does not exist her equal in the world. I know from experience we were formed to make each other happy. I have not the least expectation that I can now ever know happiness again. When you come to town, look at me, talk to me, but do not – if you can help it – exhort me, or console me.'

Another of Godwin's friends, Elizabeth Fenwick wrote two days later to Mary's younger sister, Evarina Wollstonecraft, in Dublin. 'I was with [Mary] at the time of her delivery, and with very little intermission until the moment of her death. Every skillful effort that medical knowledge of the highest class could make, was exerted to save her. It is not possible to describe the unremitting and devoted attentions of her husband ... No woman was ever more happy in marriage than Mrs Godwin. Whoever endured more anguish than Mr Godwin endures? Her description of him, in the very last moments of her recollection was, "He is the kindest, best man in the world."'

Mrs Fenwick added thoughtfully, and perhaps tactfully: 'I know of no consolation for myself, but in remembering how happy she had lately been, and how much she was admired, and almost idolized, by some of the most eminent and best of human beings.'

To take advantage of this surge of interest and sympathy across the literary world, Wollstonecraft's life-long friend and publisher, Joseph Johnson, proposed to Godwin an immediate edition of her most recent writings. This was to include most notably her long, but unfinished, novel *Maria, or The Wrongs of Woman*, which had a strong autobiographical subtext. It was a shrewd idea, to provide a fictional follow-up to Mary's most famous work of five years previously, *The Rights of Woman*. The two titles cleverly called attention to each other: 'The Rights' reinforced by 'The Wrongs'.

Though unfinished, *The Wrongs of Woman: A Fragment in Two Volumes* contained a celebration of true Romantic friendships, and a blistering attack on conventional marriage. The narrator Maria's husband has committed her to a lunatic asylum, having first brought her to court on a (false) charge of adultery. The judge's summary of Maria's case, which comes where the manuscript breaks off, ironically encapsulates many of the male prejudices that Mary Wollstonecraft had fought against all her life.

> The judge, in summing up the evidence, alluded to the fallacy of letting women plead their feelings, as an excuse for the violation of the marriage-vow. For his part, he had always determined to oppose all innovation, and the new-fangled notions that encroached on the good old rules of conduct. We did not want French principles in public or private life – and, if women were allowed to plead their feelings, as an excuse or palliation of infidelity, it was opening a flood-gate for immorality. What virtuous women thought of her feelings? – it was her duty to love and obey the man chosen by her parents and relations . . .

Johnson also suggested that Godwin should include some biographical materials. The idea for a short memorial essay by Mary's husband was mooted, as was the convention in such circumstances; and possibly a small selection from her letters.

Battling against his grief, Godwin determined do justice to his wife by editing her *Posthumous Works*. Immediately after the funeral on 15 September, he moved into Mary's own study at No.9 Polygon, surrounded himself with all her books and papers, and hung her portrait by John Opie above his desk for inspiration. He hired a housekeeper, Louisa Jones, to look after the two children who were now his responsibility: the little motherless baby Mary (the future Mary Shelley); and four-year old Fanny, who was Wollstonecraft's earlier love-child by an American, Gilbert Imlay.

Both as a father and as an author, he regarded himself as fulfilling a sacred trust, and wrote: 'It has always appeared to me, that to give the public some account of a person of eminent merit deceased, is a duty incumbent on survivors . . . The justice which is thus done to the illustrious dead, converts into the fairest source of animation and encouragement to those who would follow them in the same career.' (Preface)

2

Godwin immersed himself in papers and memories for the next three months, and writing at speed, soon found that the short essay was expanding into a full Life. He turned all his cool, scholarly methods on the supremely emotional task in hand. He reread all Mary's printed works, sorted her unpublished manuscripts, and established a precise chronology of her life from birth. He dated and meticulously numbered the 160 letters they had exchanged. He interviewed her friends in London like Johnson, and wrote to others abroad, like Hugh Skeys in Ireland. He sent diplomatic messages to Mary's estranged sister, Evarina Wollstonecraft in Dublin, requesting family letters and reminiscences. He assembled his own journal notes of their intimate conversations, and lovingly reconstructed others, such as the long September day spent walking round the garden where she had grown up near Barking, in Essex. Here Mary had suddenly begun reminiscing about her childhood.

Godwin recalled the moment tenderly, but with characteristic exactitude: 'In September 1796, I accompanied my wife in a visit to this spot. No person reviewed with great sensibility, the scenes of her childhood. We found the house uninhabited, and the garden in a wild and ruinous state. She renewed her acquaintance with the market-place, the streets, and the wharf, the latter of which we found crowded with activity.' (Chapter 1)

Godwin determined to tell each phase of her short but turbulent life with astonishing openness. This was a decision that stemmed directly from the philosophy of rational enquiry and sincerity enshrined in *Political Justice*. He would use a plain, narrative style and a frank, psychological appraisal of Mary's character and temperament. He would avoid no episode, however controversial.

He would write about the cruelty of her father (still living); the strange passionate friendship with Fanny Blood; the overbearing demands of Mary's siblings; her endless struggles for financial independence; her writer's blocks and difficulties with authorship; her enigmatic relationship with the painter Henry Fuseli; her passionate affair with the American Gilbert Imlay in Paris; her illegitimate child Fanny; her two suicide attempts; and finally their own love-affair in London, and Mary's agonizing death. This would be a revolutionary kind of intimate biography: it would tell the truth about the human condition, and particularly the truth about women's lives.

As the biography expanded, Godwin's contacts and advisors began to grow increasingly uneasy. Evarina Wollstonecraft wrote anxiously from Dublin, expressing reservations. She had been delighted at her clever elder sister's literary success, and been helped financially by it. But it now emerged that she had quarreled with Mary after her Paris adventures, and disapproved of the marriage to Godwin. She had not been properly consulted by Godwin, and feared personal disclosures and publicity. In a letter of 24 November 1797, she abruptly refused to lend Godwin any of the family correspondence, and informed him that a detailed biographical notice would be premature. She implied that it would damage her (and her sister Elizabeth's) future prospects as governesses.

> When Eliza and I first learnt your intention of publishing immediately my sister Mary's Life, we concluded that you only meant a sketch ... We thought your application to us rather premature, and had no intention of satisfying your demands till we found that [Hugh] Skeys had proffered our assistance without our knowledge ... At a future date we would willingly have given whatever information was necessary; and even now we would not have shrunk from the task, however anxious we may be to avoid reviving the recollections it would raise, or loath to fall into the pain of thoughts it must lead to, did we suppose it possible to accomplish the work you have undertaken in the time you specify.

Evarina concluded that a detailed Life was highly undesirable, and that it was impossible for Godwin to be 'even tolerably accurate' without her help. On reflection, Godwin decided to ignore these family objections. He judged them to be inspired partly by sibling jealousy, partly by the sisters' desire to control the biography for themselves, but mostly by unreasonable fear of the simple truth.

Other sources proved equally recalcitrant. Gilbert Imlay had disappeared with an actress to Paris, and could not be consulted. He had not seen Mary for over a year, though he had agreed to make a trust in favour of his little daughter Fanny. When this was not forthcoming, Godwin officially adopted her. Godwin felt that it was impossible to understand Mary's situation without telling the whole story, and now took the radical decision to publish all Mary's correspondance with Imlay, consisting of 77 love-letters written between spring 1793 and winter 1795. He convinced Johnson that these *Letters to Imlay* should occupy an additional two volumes of the *Posthumous Works*, bringing them to four in total. His *Memoirs* would now be published separately, but would also quote from this correspondance, openly naming Imlay.

The *Letters* gave only Mary's side of the correspondence (which Imlay had returned at her request). They thus left his own attitude and behaviour to be inferred. But they dramatically revealed the whole painful sequence of the affair from Mary's point of view, from her initial infatuation with Imlay in Paris to her suicidal attempts when he abandoned her in London. This was another daring, not to say reckless, publishing decision which sacrificed traditional areas of privacy to biographical truth. Godwin's own feelings as a husband were also being coolly set aside. In his Preface he described the *Letters* as 'the finest examples of the language of sentiment and passion ever presented to the world', comparable to Goethe's epistolary novel of Romantic love and suicide *The Sorrows of Young Werther* (1774). They were produced by 'a glowing imagination and a heart penetrated with the passion it essays to describe'.

Henry Fuseli briefly and non-committaly discussed Mary with Godwin, but having given him a tantalizing glimpse of a whole drawer full of her letters, refused to let him see a single one. If he knew of Godwin's intentions with regards to Mary's letters to Imlay, this is hardly surprising. But it left the exact nature of their relationship still enigmatic. Years later the Fuseli letters were seen by Godwin's own biographer, Kegan Paul (see Further Reading), who claimed that they showed intellectual admiration, but not sexual passion. Yet when these letters were eventually sold to the Shelley family (for £50), Sir Percy Shelley carefully destroyed them unpublished, towards the end of the 19th century.

Joseph Johnson was torn between a natural desire to accede to Godwin's wishes as the grieving widow, and his long-standing professional role of defending Mary's literary reputation. He may also have entertained the very understandable hope of achieving a publishing *coup*. He at least warned Godwin of several undiplomatic references to living persons in the biography, especially the aristocratic Kingsborough children to whom Mary had been a governess in Ireland, and the powerful and well-disposed Wedgwood family. He also questioned the wisdom of describing Mary's many male friendships, in London, Dublin and Paris, so unguardedly. He felt the ambiguous account of Fuseli was particularly ill-judged, and challenged Godwin's characterization of the painter's 'cynical' attitude towards Mary.

But Godwin would not give way on any of these issues. On 11th January 1798, shortly before publication, he wrote unrepentantly to Johnson, refusing to make any last minute changes. 'With respect to Mr Fuseli, I am sincerely sorry not to have pleased you . . . As to his cynical cast, his impatience of contradiction, and his propensity to satire, I have carefully observed them . . .' He added that, in his view, Mary had actually 'copied' these traits while under Fuseli's influence in 1792, and this was a significant part of her emotional development. He was committed to describing this, 'in the sincerity of my judgement', even though sometimes unfavourable to her.

This idea that Mary Wollstonecraft's intellectual power grew out of a combination of emotional strengths and weaknesses, was central to Godwin's notion of modern biography. 'Her errors were connected and interwoven with the qualities most characteristic of her genius.' He was not writing a pious family memorial, or a work of feminist hagiography, or a disembodied ideological tract. He felt he could sometimes be critical of Mary's behaviour, while always remaining passionately committed to her genius. Godwin stuck unswervingly to his belief in the exemplary value of full exposure. The truth about a human being would bring understanding, and then sympathy. 'I cannot easily prevail on myself to doubt, that the more fully we are presented with the picture and story as such persons as the subject of the following narrative, the more generally shall we feel ourselves attached to their fate, and a sympathy in their excellencies.' (Preface)

3

It appeared that Godwin could not have been more mistaken. Most readers were appalled by the *Memoirs* when they were first published at the end of January, 1798. There was no precedence for biography of this kind, and Godwin's 'naïve' candour and plain-speaking about his own wife filled them with horrid fascination.

Mary's old friend, the radical lawyer and publisher from Liverpool, William Roscoe, privately jotted these sad verses in the margin of his copy.

> Hard was thy fate in all the scenes of life
> As daughter, sister, mother, friend and wife;
> But harder still, thy fate in death we own,
> Thus mourn'd by Godwin with a heart of stone.

The *Historical Magazine* called the *Memoirs* 'the most hurtful book' of 1798. Robert Southey accused Godwin of 'a want of all feeling in stripping his dead wife naked'. *The European Magazine* described the work as 'the history of a philosophical wanton', and was sure it would be read 'with detestation by everyone attached to the interests of religion and morality; and with indignation by any one who might feel any regard for the unhappy woman, whose frailties should have been buried in oblivion.'

The Monthly Magazine, a largely conservative woman's journal, saw Mary as a kind of female Icarus figure, who had burnt out her talents with pride and ambition. 'She was a woman of high genius; and, as she felt the whole strength of her powers, she thought herself lifted, in a degree, above the ordinary travels of civil communities . . .'

The most even-handed was Johnson's own *Analytical Review*, which observed that the biography, though remarkable, lacked intellectual depth. It contained 'no correct history of the formation of Mrs G's mind. We are neither informed of her favourite books, her hours of study, nor her attainments in languages and philosophy.' Even more pointedly, it noted that anyone who also read the *Letters* would 'stand astonished at the fervour, strength and duration of her affection for Imlay'.

These initial criticisms, some written more in sorrow than in anger, and not necessarily bad publicity (at least for Johnson) were soon followed by more formidable attacks. *The Monthly*

Review, previously a supporter of Wollstonecraft's work, now in May 1798 wrote with extreme disapproval of Godwin's revelations: 'blushes would suffuse the cheeks of most husbands if they were *forced* to relate those anecdotes of their wives which Mr Godwin voluntarily proclaims to the world. The extreme eccentricity of Mr Godwin's sentiments will account for this conduct. Virtue and vice are weighed by him in a balance of his own. He neither looks to marriage with respect, nor to suicide with horror.'

The *Anti-Jacobin Review* delivered a general onslaught on the immorality that everything that Wollstonecraft was supposed to stand for: outrageous sexual behaviour, inappropriate education for young women, disrespect for parental authority, non-payment of creditors, suicidal emotionalism, repulsive rationalism, consorting with the enemy in time of war, and disbelief in God. It implied that the case was even worse than Godwin made out – 'the biographer does not mention her many amours' – and provided a helpful Index to the more offensive subject-matter of the *Memoirs*.

> Godwin edits the Posthumous Works of his wife – inculcates the promiscuous intercourse of the sexes – reprobates marriage – considers Mary Godwin a model for female imitation – certifies his wife's constitution to have been amorous – Memoirs of her – account of his wife's adventures as a kept mistress – celebrates her happiness while the concubine of Imlay – informs the public that she was concubine to himself before she was his wife – her passions inflamed by celibacy – falls in love with a married man [Fuseli] – on the breaking out of the war betakes herself to our enemies – intimate with the French leaders under Robespierre – with Thomas Paine . . .

James Gillray, quick to sense a public mood, produced one of his most savage cartoons in *The Anti-Jacobin* for August 1798. Mockingly entitled 'The New Morality', it showed a giant Cornucopia of Ignorance vomiting a stream of books into the gutter, which include Paine's *Rights of Man*, Wollstonecraft's *Wrongs of Women*, and Godwin's *Memoirs*. Godwin looks on in the guise of jackass, standing on his hind-legs and braying from a copy of *Political Justice*.

The gothic novelist Horace Walpole described Wollstonecraft as 'a Hyena in petticoats'. The polemicist and antiquarian Richard Polwhele leapt into print with an entire poem against her, entitled 'The Unsexed Females', 1798.

> See Wollstonecraft, whom no decorum checks,
> Arise, the intrepid champion of her sex;
> O'er humbled man assert the sovereign claim,
> And slight the timid blush of virgin fame . . .

The Reverend Polwhele goes on piously to enumerate her love-affairs, her illegitimate child, her suicide attempts, and her lack of religion. Furthermore, he accuses Wollstonecraft of leading astray a whole generation of blue-stockings and female intellectuals. They are 'unsex'd' (presumably like Lady Macbeth), in the sense of having abandoned their traditional role as wives and mothers. They are a 'melting tribe' of vengeful, voracious and intellectually perverted women authors, who have been seduced by Wollstonecraft's principles.

Polwhele cites them by name in what is intended as a litany of shame: Mary Hays, Mrs Barbauld, Mary Robinson, Charlotte Smith, Helen Maria Williams . . . It is also, perhaps more sinisterly, intended as a kind of 'blacklist' of politically suspect authors, whose books no respectable woman should purchase. Many of these were of course friends of Godwin's, and they do indeed represent an entire generation of 'English Jacobin' writers, for whom the American and French Revolutions had been an inspiration, and against whom the tide of history was now ineluctably turning. For many of them the paths of their professional careers would henceforth curve downwards towards poverty, exile, obscurity and premature death.

It was now open season on Godwin. Yet paradoxically the *Memoirs* were selling briskly, for a second edition was called for by the summer of 1798. There were also printings in France and America. After anxious discussion with Joseph Johnson, Godwin made a series of alterations in the text, most notably re-writing (or rather, expanding) passages connected with Henry Fuseli, Mary's suicide attempt in the Thames, and the summary of her character with which the biography concludes. These three re-written sections from the second edition, are given in the Appendix at the end of the present text.

He also suppressed the references to the Wedgwood family, and rephrased sentences that had been gleefully taken by reviewers as sexually ambiguous. But the overall character of the *Memoirs* was unchanged, and it remained an intense provocation. Other events also served fortuitously to keep up the sense of a continuing outrage against public morals. One of Mary's ex-pupils from the Kingsborough family was involved in an elopement (and murder) scandal; while Johnson himself was imprisoned for six months for publishing a seditious libel, though quite unconnected with the *Memoirs*. The sentence broke the elderly Johnson's health, and effectively ended his career as the greatest radical publisher of the day.

The *Anti-Jacobin* and other conservative magazines felt free to keep up their attacks for months, and indeed years, descending to increasing scurrility and causing Godwin endless private anguish. Three years later in August 1801, the subject was still topical enough for the young Tory George Canning to publish a long set of jeering satirical verses, entitled 'The Vision of Liberty'. It was not even necessary for Canning to give Godwin and Wollstonecraft's surnames. One stanza will suffice.

> William hath penn'd a wagon-load of stuff
> And Mary's Life at last he needs must write,
> Thinking her whoredoms were not known enough
> Till fairly printed off in black and white.
> With wond'rous glee and pride, this simple wight
> Her brothel feats of wantonness sets down;
> Being her spouse, he tells, with huge delight
> How oft she cuckolded the silly clown,
> And lent, o lovely piece!, herself to half the town.

Wollstonecraft's name was now too controversial, or even ridiculous, to mention in serious publications. Her erstwhile supporter Mary Hays omitted her from the five-volumes *Dictionary of Female Biography* that she compiled in 1803. The same astonishing omission occurs in Mathilda Bentham's *Dictionary of Celebrated Women* of 1804. Satirical attacks on Godwin and Wollstonecraft continued throughout the next decade, though many of them were now in the form of fiction.

Maria Edgeworth wrote a comic version of the Wollstonecraft

type in the person of the headstrong Harriet Freke (she promulgates adultery, intellectual repartee and female dueling) who appears in her novel *Belinda* (1801). The beautiful Amelia Alderson, now safely married to the painter John Opie (who had executed the tender portrait of Wollstonecraft that always hung in Godwin's study) revised her views on the springs of domestic happiness. Using Wollstonecraft's story, she produced a fictional account of a disastrous saga of unmarried love in *Adeline Mowbray* (1805). Much later Fanny Burney explored the emotional contradictions of Wollstonecraft's life in the long debates on matrimony and love, which are played out like elegant tennis rallies, between the sensible Juliet and the passionate Elinor, in *The Wanderer, or Female Difficulties* (1813).

Alexander Chalmers summed up the case against Wollstonecraft in his entry for *The General Biographical Dictionary* which appeared in 1814, at the very end of the Napoleonic Wars. This was a time when patriotic feeling was at its height, and distrust of subversive or vaguely French ideologies was at its most extreme. Mary Wollstonecraft was accordingly dismissed as 'a voluptuary and a sensualist'. Her views on women's rights and education were stigmatized as irrelevant fantasies: 'she unfolded many a wild theory on the duties and character of her sex.' Her whole life, as described by Godwin, was a disgusting tale best forgotten. 'She rioted in sentiments alike repugnant to religion, sense and decency'.

It is perhaps no coincidence that two years later Jane Austen's *Emma* (1816) was published to great acclaim. A new kind of heroine was being prepared for the Victorian age.

4

From this time on Mary Wollstonecraft's name was apparently eclipsed in Great Britain for the rest of the 19th century. There was only one further Victorian re-printing of *The Rights of Woman* until its centenary in 1892; and no further editions of the *Memoirs* until 1927. Respectable opinion was summed up by the formidable Harriet Martineau in her *Autobiography*, written in 1855, and published in 1870. 'Women of the Wollstonecraft order . . . do infinite mischief, and for my part, I do not wish to have anything to do with them.' She concluded that the story of her life proved that Wollstonecraft was neither 'a safe example, nor a successful champion of Woman and her Rights'.

The force and endurance of these attacks, and the sense of shock and outrage that they express, suggest that the *Memoirs* had touched on a deep nerve in British society. It had arrived at a critical moment at the end of the 1790s, when both political ideology and social fashion had turned decisively against the revolutionary hopes and freedoms that Wollstonecraft's life represented. It was a time of political reaction and social retrenchment. It was also wartime.

As William Hazlitt later wrote of Godwin: 'The Spirit of the Age was never more fully shown than in the treatment of this writer – its love of paradox and change, its dastard submission to prejudice and the fashion of the day . . . Fatal reverse! Is truth then so variable? Is it one thing at twenty and another at forty? Is it at a burning heat in 1793, and below zero in 1814?' (*The Spirit of the Age*, 1825)

It is now possible to see a little more clearly what made the *Memoirs* so provocative and so remarkable. No one had written about a woman like this before, except perhaps Daniel Defoe in the fictional Lives of his incorrigible 18th century heroines, like Moll Flanders. But Godwin was writing strict and indeed meticulous non-fiction, using a plain narrative style and a fearless psychological acuity. He signally ignored, or even deliberately aimed to provoke, proprieties of every kind, especial political and sexual ones.

Beginning with her uncertain birth in 1759 (Mary was unsure whether she was born in Spitalfields or Epping Forest), Godwin unflinchingly describes her restless and unhappy childhood, dominated by a drunken, bullying and abusive father, and a spoilt elder brother. His account gives the famous and iconic picture of Mary sleeping all night on the floor outside the parental bedroom, hoping to protect her mother from her father's assaults. This upbringing left her the victim of life-long depressive episodes, alternating with periods of reckless energy and anger. 'Mary was a very good hater'. But she was determined on a life-long 'project of personal independence', and revealed an instinctive desire to control and manage those around her. (Chapter 1).

He next recounts her overwhelming and 'fervent' friendship for the beautiful Fanny Blood, 'which for years constituted the ruling passion of her mind'. Godwin has no reservations in proclaiming how deeply those feelings shaped her emotional life in her twenties, and it is here that he first makes the notorious comparison between Mary and Goethe's lovelorn young Werther. The friendship took her on her first remarkable voyage, to Portugal in 1785, where Fanny died in childbirth. This passion was never subsequently forgotten. (Chapter 2 and 3)

The atheist Godwin also sympathetically describes and analyses Mary's religious beliefs. He treats them in a strikingly modern and psychological way, less as the product of Christian dogma or 'polemical discussion', but more as an imaginative expression of her temperament and character. 'She found inexpressible delight in the beauties of nature, and in the splendid reveries of the imagination . . . When she walked amidst the wonders of nature, she was accustomed to converse with her God.' (Chapter 3)

Next comes her combative experiences as a governess in Ireland, and the discovery of her charismatic talents as a teacher, and gifts as an educational writer (Chapter 4). This is followed from 1788 by the excitement of her early freelance work in London, and her professional friendship with the publisher Joseph Johnson, during which an intense period of self-education takes place. At the same time she takes responsibilty for the careers and financing of most of her family, including her sisters and her father. (Chapter 5).

Then in 1792, at the age of 35, and at a climactic moment in revolutionary history, she achieves the rapid and triumphant writing of *The Rights of Woman*, in which she brings both her wide reading and her bitter personal experiences to bear, and makes herself in Godwin's words 'the effectual champion' of her sex. (Chapter 6). Yet at the very moment of success, she is frustrated and humiliated by the ill-judged affair with the married (but bisexual) painter Henry Fuseli, whose exact nature Godwin leaves curiously ill-defined

It is exactly at this crucial half-way point in his narrative, and significantly just out of chronological sequence, that Godwin ironically places his first and deeply unsatisfactory meeting with Mary, at a dinner party with Johnson and Tom Paine in November 1791. Far from being love at first sight, they quarrel so fiercely that Paine hardly gets a word in edgeways. It is again typical of Godwin that he does not omit this memorable scene.

From now on the biography seems to accelerate and intensify. Mary sets out on her own to observe events in revolutionary Paris, and as the Terror begins, falls in love with the handsome American adventurer Gilbert Imlay. Godwin's description of her sexual awakening by Imlay, using the beautiful pre-Freudian imagery of 'a serpent on a rock', is one of his triumphs as a biographer, and one wonders how much it must have cost him. Here the comparison with the suicidal young Werther is also repeated. (Chapter 7).

Mary is registered as Imlay's wife, and in 1794 bears his illegitimate child – named Fanny (after Fanny Blood) – in Le Havre-Marat. She embarks on a desperate journey to Scandinavia, transforming a secret business venture for Imlay into a wonderful, melancholy book of Romantic travels. Godwin's tender account of his personal reaction to this book, prepares the ground for the unexpected love-match that will follow.

> If ever there was a book calculated to make a man in love with its author, this appears to me to be the book. She speaks of her sorrows, in a way that fills us with melancholy, and dissolves us in tenderness, at the same time that she displays a genius which commands our full attention.' (Chapter 8)

On Mary's return to London in 1795, she discovers that she is betrayed by Imlay, and twice tries to commit suicide, first with an overdose of opium and then by jumping into the Thames. Godwin's vivid and moving account of this episode includes another unforgettable image of Mary, pacing Putney Bridge at night in the rain, hoping that by soaking her clothes she would drown more quickly. Paradoxically, it opened Godwin to the charge of trying to make a moral defence of suicide. (Chapter 8).

The remaining two chapters become increasingly confessional. Yet they are written in the same admirably limpid and economic style, in which understatement is deliberately used to contain overwhelming emotion. Godwin describes how they fell in love in the spring of 1796, and began sleeping together in August, long before their mutual decision to marry. This was only taken after Mary became pregnant. Such a candid admission also opened Godwin to further mockery and abuse, although he never altered it in the second edition. (Chapter 9).

Finally, at great length and in almost gynecological detail, without the least reference to the traditional comforts of religion, Godwin painfully and minutely describes Mary's death, eleven days after bearing her second child (Chapter 10). It was the first time a deathbed had been described in this intimate way, including such unsettling details as Mary being given puppies to draw off her breast-milk, and being given too much wine to dull her pain.

5

Some two centuries later its is still possible to find the *Memoirs* shocking, and to disagree about the picture its draws of Wollstonecraft. Many feminist critics believe that it miscast her as a Romantic heroine, and fatally undervalued her intellectual powers. Most of her modern biographers freely use Godwin as wonderful source material, but condemn him as a hopelessly biased witness.

Even an outstandingly perceptive and measured writer like Claire Tomalin is uneasy about the effect of his work. 'In their own way, even the *Memoirs* had diminished and distorted Mary's real importance: by minimizing her claim to be taken seriously for her ideas, and presenting her instead as a female Werther, a romantic and tragic heroine, he may have been giving the truth as he wanted to see it, but was very far from serving the cause she had believed in. He made no attempt to discuss her intellectual development, and he was unwilling to consider the validity of her feminist ideas in any detail.' (Tomalin, 1974)

This has weight, and is curiously close to the criticism originally made by the *Analytical Review* in 1798. But it has to be set, for example, against Godwin's extended analysis and celebration of the significance of *The Rights of Woman* in Chapter 6. 'Never did any author enter into a cause, with more ardent desire to be found, not a flourishing and empty declaimer, but an effectual champion . . . When we consider the importance of its doctrines, and the eminence of genius it displays, it seems not very improbable that [her book] will be read as long as the English language endures . . .'

Much criticism has also been directed against Godwin's attempt at the very end of his biography, to summarize Mary's 'intellectual character', and apparently draw a 'gendered' distinction between masculine and feminine intelligence. He contrasts his own cool rational delight in 'logic and metaphysical distinction', with her strong, warm emotional instincts and 'taste for the picturesque'. (Chapter 10). This is easily ridiculed. But it is overlooked that Godwin, the faithful biographer, was actually paraphrasing one of Wollstonecraft's own letters to him of August 1796. This is what Mary herself wrote on the subject.

> Our imaginations have been rather differently employed – I am more a painter than you – I like to tell the truth, my taste for the picturesque has been more cultivated . . . My affections have been more exercised than yours, I believe, and my senses are quick, without the aid of fancy – yet tenderness always prevails, which inclines me to be angry with myself when, I do not animate and please those I love.

But the problem of the intimate biography which seems to violate certain codes of family loyalty and trust is still with us. Thirty years ago, Nigel Nicolson's *Portrait of a Marriage* (1973), which revealed his mother Vita Sackville-West's lesbian relationships, and his father's homosexual ones, raised such questions. More recently, John Bailey's account of his wife Iris Murdoch's relentless destruction by Alzheimer's disease, in *Iris* (1999), left many readers and reviewers deeply troubled by such revelations. Yet both these are fine books, and it seems possible that biography as a form is destined to challenge conventions of silence and ignorance.

One also has to consider the historical effect of such a powerful biography is a more oblique way. The fact, for example, that Mary's life inspired so many Romantic novels, suggests Godwin had also made her something of a legendary figure. The emotional intensity of Marianne Dashwood in *Sense and Sensibility*, the novel which Jane Austen originally drafted at just this time (1797–8), might owe more than we suspect to Mary's example.

Her outrageous or comic persona still contained heroic or exemplary possibilities. Harriet Freke might yet be reincarnated as J.S. Mill's feminist companion Harriet Taylor, who was largely responsible for Mill's great work *On the Subjection of Women* (1869). Wollstonecraft was championed by the reformer Robert Owen, and written about admiringly in a little-known essay by George Eliot. In 1885 she was one of the first figures to be included in the *Eminent Woman Series*, alongside Elizabeth Fry and Mary Lamb.

So there is an alternative tradition in which Mary Wollstonecraft's reputation. runs underground through the 19th century, especially among women writers. It has been traced in a recent classic of feminist scholarship, *Wollstonecraft's Daughters*, 1996. (See Further Reading)

It eventually resurfaces in the superb essay by Virginia Woolf of 1932. Inspired by the tone of the *Memoirs*, she describes Gilbert Imlay not as a villain but as a laughable fool: 'tickling for minnows he hooked a dolphin'. She celebrates Mary's relationship with Godwin as the 'most fruitful experiment' of her life. Their marriage was 'an experiment, as Mary's life had been an experiment from the start, an attempt to make human conventions conform more closely to human needs.' In a striking and prophetic conclusion, Woolf sees the story and example of Mary's tempestuous life blossoming again among her contemporaries. 'She is alive and active, she argues and experiments, we hear her voice and trace her influence even now among the living.'.

6

Perhaps it was there from the beginning. A year after the publication of the *Memoirs*, the poet and novelist Mary Robinson released her *Letter to the Women of England on the Injustice of Mental Subordination* (1799). Originally a Shakespearean actress ('Perdita' Robinson) and mistress to the teenage Prince of Wales, Robinson's later literary work in the 1790s brought her the friendship of both Godwin and Coleridge. Her *Letter* initially appeared under the pseudonym 'Anne Randall', but it was published by Longman, the biggest bookseller in London, and received wide circulation.

Robinson refers openly and admiringly to *The Rights of Woman* and salutes Wollstonecraft as 'an illustrious British female ... to whose genius Posterity will render justice'. In a militant footnote she describes herself proudly as 'avowedly of the same school' as Mary Wollstonecraft, and prophetically foresees her embattled life as having initiated a long campaign for women's rights which would stretch far into the 19th century.

'For it requires *a legion of Wollstonecrafts* to undermine the poisons of prejudice and malevolence.'

One of Mary Robinson's most striking conclusions at the end of her hundred page *Letter* is that Wollstonecraft's commitment to female education (emphasized by Godwin) lead logically to the idea of women going to university. 'Had fortune enabled me, I would build a UNIVERSITY FOR WOMEN.' Only then would women truly be equal.

In the year after Wollstonecraft's death, a new biographical series entitled *Public Characters* (dedicated to the King) was launched, and would continue for the next decade. It carried some 30 'living biographies' per annual issue, and featured such figures as Nelson, Wilberforce, Humphry Davy, Sheridan and Castlereagh. Volume 2 (1799) included a twenty-page 'contemporary biography' of Godwin. It was warmly favourable, and gave a sympathetic four page account of his marriage to Mary Wollstonecraft ('that most celebrated and most injured woman'), and unstinting praise for both editions of the *Memoirs*. It concluded as follows, in a remarkable passage that has never been reprinted since.

It was in January 1798 that Mr Godwin published his *Memoirs* of the Life of Mrs Godwin. In May of the same year a second edition of that work appeared. A painful choice seems to present itself to every ingenuous person who composes Memoirs of himself or of any one so nearly connected with himself as in the present instance. He must either express himself with disadvantage to the illiberal and malicious temper that exists in the world, or violate the honor and integrity of his feelings.

Yet that the heart should be known in all its windings, is an object of infinite importance to him who would benefit the human race. Mr Godwin did not prefer a cowardly silence, nor treachery to the public, having chosen to write. Perhaps such works as the *Memoirs* of Mrs Godwin's Life, and Rousseau's *Confessions*, will ever disgrace their writers with the meaner spirits of the world. But then it is to be remembered, that this herd neither confers, nor can take away, fame.'

Most moving of all, the revolutionary influence of Mary Wollstonecraft's life continued through the next generation of her own family, the family she never knew. It was a powerful and unsettling example. Her love-child, Fanny Imlay, eventually committed suicide. But when her daughter Mary Godwin and Shelley eloped to France in 1814, they carried the *Posthumous Works* and the *Memoirs* with them in their tiny travelling trunk, and read them during their first nights in Paris. Shelley's poem *The Revolt of Islam* (1817) contained a heroic portrait of her. His triumphant chorus from his late verse drama *Hellas* (1821), written about the Greek War of Independence, drew on Godwin's memorable snake imagery of hope and revival.

> The world's great age begins anew,
> The golden years return,
> The earth does like a snake renew
> Her winter weeds outworn . . .

Mary Shelley's entire literary career was inspired by her mother's example, and especially perhaps her desire to write novels of ideas. Both *Frankenstein* (1818), and *The Last Man* (1826) can be seen as part of the complex Wollstonecraft inheritance. After her father Godwin's death, she always intended to write a combined biography of both her daring literary parents.

A few scattered manuscript notes alone have survived, probably dating from the early 1840s. This is what the subdued, widowed, middle-aged Victorian Mary Shelley wrote about her outrageous mother Mary Wollstonecraft. 'Her genius was undeniable. She had been bred in the hard school of adversity, and having experienced the sorrows entailed on the poor and oppressed, an earnest desire was kindled within her to diminish these sorrows. Her sound understanding, her intrepidity, her sensibility and eager sympathy, stamped all her writings with force and truth, and endorsed them with a tender charm that enchants while it enlightens. She was one whom all loved, who had ever seen her.'

But of course Mary had never seen her mother. She only knew and loved her through her own writings and her father's intrepid and controversial *Memoirs*. Such is the dangerous, enduring power of biography.

The text of the Memoirs *reprinted here is that of Godwin's first, uncorrected edition of January 1798, apart from a few spellings that have been modernized. The three passages that Godwin substantially re-wrote for the second edition − concerning Henry Fuseli (Chapter 6), Wollstonecraft's suicide attempt (Chapter 8), and his summary of Wollstonecraft's character (Chapter 10) − are given in the Appendix.*

SELECT CHRONOLOGY

Wollstonecraft publishes *Letters Written during a Short Residence in Norway, Denmark and Sweden*

1796   (April) Wollstonecraft calls upon Godwin

1797   (March) Godwin and Wollstonecraft marry
(30 August) Birth of Mary Godwin
(10 September) Death of Mary Wollstonecraft

1798   (January) Godwin publishes *Memoirs of the Author of the Rights of Woman* (first edition)
(August) Godwin publishes *Memoirs* (second edition)

1801   Godwin publishes *St Leon* (novel)

1814   Shelley elopes with Mary Godwin

1816   Fanny Imlay (Godwin) commits suicide

1836   Death of William Godwin

1853   Death of Mary Shelley

1892   Centenary edition of *A Vindication of the Rights of Women*

1927   Third edition of *Memoirs*, edited by William Clark Durant

MEMOIRS OF
THE AUTHOR OF
'THE RIGHTS OF WOMAN'

PREFACE

It has always appeared to me, that to give the public some account of the life of a person of eminent merit deceased, is a duty incumbent on survivors. It seldom happens that such a person passes through life, without being the subject of thoughtless calumny, or malignant misrepresentation. It cannot happen that the public at large should be on a footing with their intimate acquaintance, and be the observer of those virtues which discover themselves principally in personal intercourse. Every benefactor of mankind is more or less influenced by a liberal passion for fame; and survivors only pay a debt due to these benefactors, when they assert and establish on their part, the honour they loved. The justice which is thus done to the illustrious dead, converts into the fairest source of animation and encouragement to those who would follow them in the same career. The human species at large is interested in this justice, as it teaches them to place their respect and affection, upon those qualities which best deserve to be esteemed and loved. I cannot easily prevail on myself to doubt, that the more fully we are presented with the picture and story of such persons as the subject of the following narrative, the more generally shall we feel in ourselves an attachment to their fate, and a sympathy in their excellencies. There are not many individuals with whose character the public welfare and improvement are more intimately connected, than the author of *A Vindication of the Rights of Woman*.

The facts detailed in the following pages, are principally taken from the mouth of the person to whom they relate; and of the veracity and ingenuousness of her habits, perhaps no one that was ever acquainted with her, entertains a doubt. The writer of this narrative, when he has met with persons, that in any degree created to themselves an interest and attachment in his mind, has always felt a curiosity to be acquainted with the scenes through which they had passed, and the incidents that had contributed to form their understandings and character. Impelled by this sentiment, he repeatedly led the conversation of Mary to topics of this sort; and, once or twice, he made notes in her presence, of a few dates calculated to arrange the circumstances in his mind. To the materials thus collected, he has added an industrious enquiry among the persons most intimately acquainted with her at the different periods of her life.

CHAPTER ONE

1759–1775

M ary Wollstonecraft was born on the 27th of April 1759. Her father's name was Edward John, and the name of her mother Elizabeth, of the family of Dixons of Ballyshannon in the kingdom of Ireland: her paternal grandfather was a respectable manufacturer in Spitalfields, and is supposed to have left to his son a property of about 10,000*l*. Three of her brothers and two sisters are still living; their names, Edward, James, Charles, Eliza, and Everina. Of these, Edward only was older than herself; he resides in London. James is in Paris, and Charles in or near Philadelphia in America. Her sisters have for some years been engaged in the office of governesses in private families, and are both at present in Ireland.

I am doubtful whether the father of Mary was bred to any profession; but, about the time of her birth, he resorted, rather perhaps as an amusement than a business, to the occupation of farming. He was of a very active, and somewhat versatile disposition, and so frequently changed his abode, as to throw some ambiguity upon the place of her birth. She told me, that the doubt in her mind in that respect, lay between London, and a farm upon Epping Forest, which was the principal scene of the five first years of her life.

Mary was distinguished in early youth, by some portion of that exquisite sensibility, soundness of understanding, and decision of character, which were the leading features of her mind through the whole course of her life. She experienced in the first period of her existence, but few of those indulgences and marks of affection, which are principally calculated to soothe the subjection and sorrows of our early years. She was not the favourite either of her father or mother. Her father was a man of a quick, impetuous disposition, subject to alternate fits of kindness and cruelty. In his family he was a despot, and his wife appears to have been the first, and most submissive of his subjects. The mother's partiality was fixed upon the eldest son, and her system of government relative to Mary, was characterized by considerable rigour. She, at length, became convinced of her mistake, and adopted a different plan with her younger daughters. When, in the *Wrongs of Woman*, Mary speaks of 'the petty cares which obscured the morning of her heroine's life; continual restraint in the most trivial matters; unconditional submission to orders, which, as a mere child, she soon discovered to be unreasonable, because inconsistent and contradictory; and the being often obliged to sit, in the presence of her parents, for three or four hours together, without daring to utter a word;' she is, I believe, to be considered as copying the outline of the first period of her own existence.

But it was in vain that the blighting winds of unkindness or indifference, seemed destined to counteract the superiority of Mary's mind. It surmounted every obstacle; and by degrees, from a person little considered in the family, she became in some sort its director and umpire. The despotism of her education cost her many a heart-ache. She was not formed to be the contented and unresisting subject of a despot; but I have heard her remark more than once, that, when she felt she had done wrong, the reproof or chastisement of her mother, instead of being a terror to her, she found to be the only thing capable of reconciling her to herself. The blows of her father, on the contrary, which were the mere ebullitions of a passionate temper, instead of humbling her roused her indignation. Upon such occasions she felt her superiority, and was apt to betray marks of contempt. The quickness of her father's temper, led him sometimes to threaten similar violence towards his wife. When that was the case, Mary would often throw herself between the despot and his victim, with the purpose to receive upon her own person the blows that might be directed against her mother. She has even laid whole nights upon the landing-place near their chamber-door, when, mistakenly, or with reason, she apprehended that her father might break out into paroxysms of violence. The conduct he held towards the members of his family, was of the same kind as that he observed towards animals. He was for the most part extravagantly fond of them; but, when he was displeased, and this frequently happened, and for very trivial reasons, his anger was alarming. Mary was what Dr Johnson would have called, 'a very good hater.' In some instance of passion exercised by her father to one of his dogs, she was accustomed to speak of her emotions of abhorrence, as having risen to agony. In a word, her conduct during her girlish years, was such, as to extort some portion of affection from her mother, and to hold her father in considerable awe.

In one respect, the system of education of the mother appears to have had merit. All her children were vigorous and healthy. This seems very much to depend upon the management of our infant years. It is affirmed by some persons of the present day, most profoundly skilled in the sciences of health and disease, that there is no period of human life so little subject to mortality, as the period of infancy. Yet, from the mismanagement to which children are exposed, many of the diseases of childhood are rendered fatal, and more persons die in that, than in any other period of human life. Mary had projected a work upon this subject, which she had carefully considered, and well understood. She has indeed left a specimen of her skill in this respect in her eldest daughter, three years and a half old, who is a singular example of vigorous constitution and florid health. Mr Anthony Carlisle, surgeon, of Soho-square, whom to name is sufficiently to honour, had promised to revise her production. This is but one out of numerous projects of activity and usefulness, which her untimely death has fatally terminated.

The rustic situation in which Mary spent her infancy, no doubt contributed to confirm the stamina of her constitution. She sported in the open air, and amidst the picturesque and refreshing scenes of nature, for which she always retained the most exquisite relish. Dolls and the other amusements usually appropriated to female children, she held in contempt; and felt a much greater propensity to join in the active and hardy sports of her brothers, than to confine herself to those of her own sex.

About the time that Mary completed the fifth year of her

age, her father removed to a small distance from his former habitation and took a farm near the Whalebone upon Epping Forest, a little way out of the Chelmsford road. In Michaelmas 1765, he once more changed his residence, and occupied a convenient house behind the town of Barking in Essex, eight miles from London. In this situation some of their nearest neighbours were, Bamber Gascoyne, esquire, successively Member of Parliament of several boroughs, and his brother, Mr Joseph Gascoyne. Bamber Gascoyne resided but little on this spot; but his brother was almost a constant inhabitant, and his family in habits of the most frequent intercourse with the family of Mary. Here Mr Wollstonecraft remained for three years. In September 1796, I accompanied my wife in a visit to this spot. No person reviewed with greater sensibility, the scenes of her childhood. We found the house uninhabited, and the garden in a wild and ruinous state. She renewed her acquaintance with the market-place, the streets, and the wharf, the latter of which we found crowded with barges, and full of activity.

In Michaelmas 1768, Mr Wollstonecraft again removed to a farm near Beverley in Yorkshire. Here the family remained for six years, and consequently, Mary did not quit this residence until she had attained the age of fifteen years and five months. The principal part of her school-education passed during this period; but it was not to any advantage of infant literature, that she was indebted for her subsequent eminence; her education in this respect was merely such, as was afforded by the day-schools of the place, in which she resided. To her recollections Beverley appeared a very handsome town, surrounded by genteel families, and with a brilliant assembly. She was surprized, when she visited it in 1795, upon her voyage to Norway, to find the reality so very much below the picture in her imagination.

Hitherto Mr Wollstonecraft had been a farmer; but the restlessness of his disposition would not suffer him to content himself with the occupation in which for some years he had been engaged, and the temptation of a commercial speculation of some sort being held out to him, he removed to a house in Queen's-Row, in Hoxton near London, for the purpose of its execution. Here he remained for a year and a half; but, being frustrated in his expectations of profit, he, after that term, gave up the project in which he was engaged, and returned to his former pursuits. During this residence in Hoxton, the writer of these memoirs inhabited, as a student, at the dissenting college in that place. It is perhaps a question of curious speculation to enquire, what would have been the amount of the difference in the pursuits and enjoyments of each party, if they had met, and considered each other with the same distinguishing regard in 1776, as they were afterwards impressed with in the year 1796. The writer had then completed the twentieth, and Mary the seventeenth year of her age. Which would have been predominant; the disadvantages of obscurity, and the pressure of a family; or the gratifications and improvement that might have flowed from their intercourse?

One of the acquaintances Mary formed at this time was with a Mr Clare, who inhabited the next house to that which was tenanted by her father, and to whom she was probably in some degree indebted for the early cultivation of her mind. Mr Clare was a clergyman, and appears to have been a humourist of a very singular cast. In his person he was deformed and delicate;

and his figure, I am told, bore a resemblance to that of the celebrated Pope. He had a fondness for poetry, and was not destitute of taste. His manners were expressive of a tenderness and benevolence, the demonstrations of which appeared to have been somewhat too artificially cultivated. His habits were those of a perfect recluse. He seldom went out of his drawing-room, and he showed to a friend of Mary a pair of shoes, which had served him, he said, for fourteen years. Mary frequently spent days and weeks together, at the house of Mr Clare.

CHAPTER TWO

1775–1783

B ut a connection more memorable originated about this time, between Mary and a person of her own sex, for whom she contracted a friendship so fervent, as for years to have constituted the ruling passion of her mind. The name of this person was Frances Blood; she was two years older than Mary. Her residence was at that time at Newington Butts, a village near the southern extremity of the metropolis; and the original instrument for bringing these two friends acquainted, was Mrs Clare, wife of the gentleman already mentioned, who was on a footing of considerable intimacy with both parties. The acquaintance of Fanny, like that of Mr Clare, contributed to ripen the immature talents of Mary.

The situation in which Mary was introduced to her, bore a resemblance to the first interview of Werter with Charlotte. She was conducted to the door of a small house, but furnished with peculiar neatness and propriety. The first object that caught her sight, was a young woman of a slender and elegant form, and eighteen years of age, busily employed in feeding and managing some children, born of the same parents, but considerably inferior to her in age. The impression Mary received from this spectacle was indelible; and, before the interview was concluded, she had taken, in her heart, the vows of an eternal friendship.

Fanny was a young woman of extraordinary accomplishments. She sung and played with taste. She drew with exquisite fidelity and neatness; and, by the employment of this talent, for some time maintained her father, mother, and family, but ultimately ruined her health by her extraordinary exertions. She read and wrote with considerable application; and the same ideas of minute and delicate propriety followed her in these, as in her other occupations.

Mary, a wild, but animated and aspiring girl of sixteen, contemplated Fanny, in the first instance, with sentiments of inferiority and reverence. Though they were much together, yet, the distance of their habitations being considerable, they supplied the want of more frequent interviews by an assiduous correspondence. Mary found Fanny's letters better spelt and better indited than her own, and felt herself abashed. She had hitherto paid but a superficial attention to literature. She had read, to gratify the ardour of an inextinguishable thirst of knowledge; but she had not thought of writing as an art. Her ambition to excel was now awakened, and she applied herself with passion and earnestness. Fanny undertook to be her instructor; and, so far as related to accuracy and method, her lessons were given with considerable skill.

It has already been mentioned that, in the spring of the year 1776, Mr Wollstonecraft quitted his situation at Hoxton, and returned to his former agricultural pursuits. The situation upon which he now fixed was in Wales, a circumstance that was felt as a severe blow to Mary's darling spirit of friendship. The principal acquaintance of the Wollstonecrafts in this retirement, was the family of a Mr Allen, two of whose daughters are since married to the two elder sons of the celebrated English potter, Josiah Wedgwood.

Wales however was Mr Wollstonecraft's residence for little more than a year. He returned to the neighbourhood of London; and Mary, whose spirit of independence was unalterable, had influence enough to determine his choice in favour of the village of Walworth, that she might be near her chosen friend. It was probably before this, that she had once or twice started the idea of quitting her parental roof, and providing for herself. But she was prevailed upon to resign this idea, and conditions were stipulated with her, relative to her having an apartment in the house that should be exclusively her own, and her commanding the other requisites of study. She did not however think herself fairly treated in these instances, and either the conditions above-mentioned, or some others, were not observed in the sequel, with the fidelity she expected. In one case, she had procured an eligible situation, and every thing was settled respecting her removal to it, when the intreaties and tears of her mother led her to surrender her own inclinations, and abandon the engagement.

These however were only temporary delays. Her propensities continued the same, and the motives by which she was instigated were unabated. In the year 1778, she being nineteen years of age, a proposal was made to her of living as a companion with a Mrs Dawson of Bath, a widow lady, with one son already adult. Upon enquiry she found that Mrs Dawson was a woman of great peculiarity of temper, that she had had a variety of companions in succession, and that no one had found it practicable to continue with her. Mary was not discouraged by this information and accepted the situation, with a resolution that she would effect in this respect, what none of her predecessors had been able to do. In the sequel she had reason to consider the account she had received as sufficiently accurate, but she did not relax in her endeavours. By method, constancy and firmness, she found the means of making her situation tolerable; and Mrs Dawson would occasionally confess, that Mary was the only person that had lived with her in that situation, in her treatment of whom she had felt herself under any restraint.

With Mrs Dawson she continued to reside for two years, and only left her, summoned by the melancholy circumstance of her mother's rapidly declining health. True to the calls of humanity, Mary felt in this intelligence an irresistible motive, and eagerly returned to the paternal roof, which she had before resolutely quitted. The residence of her father at this time, was at Enfield near London. He had, I believe, given up agriculture from the time of his quitting Wales, it appearing that he now made it less a source of profit than loss, and being thought advisable that he should rather live upon the interest of his property already in possession.

The illness of Mrs Wollstonecraft was lingering, but hopeless. Mary was assiduous in her attendance upon her mother. At first, every attention was received with acknowledgments and gratitude; but, as the attentions grew habitual, and the health of the mother more and more wretched, they were rather exacted, than received. Nothing would be taken by the unfortunate patient, but from the hands of Mary; rest was denied night or day, and by the time nature was exhausted in the parent, the daughter was qualified to assume her place, and become in turn herself a patient. The last words her mother ever uttered were, 'A little patience, and all will be over!' and these words are repeatedly referred to by Mary in the course of her writings.

Upon the death of Mrs Wollstonecraft, Mary bid final adieu to the roof of her father. According to my memorandums, I find her next the inmate of Fanny at Walham Green, near the village of Fulham. Upon what plan they now lived together I am unable to ascertain; certainly not that of Mary becoming in any degree an additional burthen upon the industry of her friend. Thus situated, their intimacy ripened; they approached more nearly to a footing of equality; and their attachment became more rooted and active.

Mary was ever ready at the call of distress, and, in particular, during her whole life was eager and active to promote the welfare of every member of her family. In 1780 she attended the deathbed of her mother; in 1782 she was summoned by a not less melancholy occasion, to attend her sister Eliza, married to a Mr Bishop, who, subsequently to a dangerous lying-in, remained for some months in a very afflicting situation. Mary continued with her sister without intermission, to her perfect recovery.

CHAPTER THREE

1783–1785

Mary was now arrived at the twenty-fourth year of her age. Her project, five years before, had been personal independence; it was now usefulness. In the solitude of attendance on her sister's illness, and during the subsequent convalescence, she had had leisure to ruminate upon purposes of this sort. Her expanded mind led her to seek something more arduous than the mere removal of personal vexations; and the sensibility of her heart would not suffer her to rest in solitary gratifications. The derangement of her father's affairs daily became more and more glaring; and a small independent provision made for herself and her sisters, appears to have been sacrificed in the wreck. For ten years, from 1782 to 1792, she may be said to have been, in a great degree, the victim of a desire to promote the benefit of others. She did not foresee the severe disappointment with which an exclusive purpose of this sort is pregnant; she was inexperienced enough to lay a stress upon the consequent gratitude of those she benefited; and she did not sufficiently consider that, in proportion as we involve ourselves in the interests and society of others, we acquire a more exquisite sense of their defects, and are tormented with their untractableness and folly.

The project upon which she now determined, was no other than that of a day-school, to be superintended by Fanny Blood, herself, and her two sisters. They accordingly opened one in the year 1783, at the village of Islington; but in the course of a few months removed it to Newington Green.

Here Mary formed some acquaintances who influenced the future events of her life. The first of these in her own estimation, was Dr Richard Price, well known for his political and mathematical calculations, and universally esteemed by those who knew him, for the simplicity of his manners, and the ardour of his benevolence. The regard conceived by these two persons for each other, was mutual, and partook of a spirit of the purest attachment. Mary had been bred in the principles of the church of England, but her esteem for this venerable preacher led her occasionally to attend upon his public instructions. Her religion was, in reality, little allied to any system of forms; and, as she has often told me, was founded rather in taste, than in the niceties of polemical discussion. Her mind constitutionally attached itself to the sublime and the amiable. She found an inexpressible delight in the beauties of nature, and in the splendid reveries of the imagination. But nature itself, she thought, would be no better than a vast blank, if the mind of the observer did not supply it with an animating soul. When she walked amidst the wonders of nature, she was accustomed to converse with her God. To her mind he was pictured as not less amiable, generous and kind, than great, wise and exalted. In fact, she had received few lessons of religion in her youth, and her religion was almost entirely of her own creation. But she was not on that account the less attached to it, or the less scrupulous in discharging what she considered as its duties. She could not recollect the time when she had believed the doctrine of future punishments. The tenets of her system were the growth of her own moral taste, and her religion therefore had always been a gratification, never a terror, to her. She expected a future state; but she would not allow her ideas of that future state to be modified by the notions of judgment and retribution. From this sketch, it is sufficiently evident, that the pleasure she took in an occasional attendance upon the sermons of Dr Price, was not accompanied with a superstitious adherence to his doctrines. The fact is, that, as far down as the year 1787, she regularly frequented public worship, for the most part according to the forms of the Church of England. After that period her attendance became less constant, and in no long time was wholly discontinued. I believe it may be admitted as a maxim, that no person of a well furnished mind, that has shaken off the implicit subjection of youth, and is not the zealous partizan of a sect, can bring himself to conform to the public and regular routine of sermons and prayers.

Another of the friends she acquired at this period, was Mrs Burgh, widow of the author of the *Political Disquisitions*, a woman universally well spoken of for the warmth and purity of her benevolence. Mary, whenever she had occasion to allude to her, to the last period of her life, paid the tribute due to her virtues. The only remaining friend necessary to be enumerated in this place, is the Rev. John Hewlet, now master of a boarding-school at Shacklewel near Hackney, whom I shall have occasion to mention hereafter.

It was during her residence at Newington Green, that she

was introduced to the acquaintance of Dr Johnson, who was at that time considered as in some sort the father of English literature. The doctor treated her with particular kindness and attention, had a long conversation with her, and desired her to repeat her visit often. This she firmly purposed to do; but the news of his last illness, and then of his death, intervened to prevent her making a second visit.

I have already said that Fanny's health had been materially injured by her incessant labours for the maintenance of her family. She had also suffered a disappointment, which preyed upon her mind. To these different sources of ill health she became gradually a victim; and at length discovered all the symptoms of a pulmonary consumption. By the medical men that attended her, she was advised to try the effects of a southern climate; and, about the beginning of the year 1785, sailed for Lisbon.

The first feeling with which Mary had contemplated her friend, was a sentiment of inferiority and reverence; but that, from the operation of a ten years' acquaintance, was considerably changed. Fanny had originally been far before her in literary attainments; this disparity no longer existed. In whatever degree Mary might endeavour to free herself from the delusions of self-esteem, this period of observation upon her own mind and that of her friend, could not pass, without her perceiving that there were some essential characteristics of genius, which she possessed, and in which her friend was deficient. The principal of these was a firmness of mind, an unconquerable greatness of soul, by which, after a short internal struggle, she was accustomed to rise above difficulties and suffering. Whatever Mary undertook, she perhaps in all instances accomplished; and, to her lofty spirit, scarcely any thing she desired, appeared hard to perform. Fanny, on the contrary, was a woman of a timid and irresolute nature, accustomed to yield to difficulties, and probably priding herself in this morbid softness of her temper. One instance that I have heard Mary relate of this sort, was that, at a certain time, Fanny, dissatisfied with her domestic situation, expressed an earnest desire to have a home of her own. Mary, who felt nothing more pressing than to relieve the inconveniences of her friend, determined to accomplish this object for her. It cost her infinite exertions; but at length she was able to announce to Fanny that a house was prepared, and that she was on the spot to receive her. The answer which Fanny returned to the letter of her friend, consisted almost wholly of an enumeration of objections to the quitting her family, which she had not thought of before, but which now appeared to her of considerable weight.

The judgment which experience had taught Mary to form of the mind of her friend, determined her in the advice she gave, at the period to which I have brought down the story. Fanny was recommended to seek a softer climate, but she had no funds to defray the expense of such an undertaking. At this time Mr Hugh Skeys of Dublin, but then resident in the kingdom of Portugal, paid his addresses to her. The state of her health Mary considered as such as scarcely to afford the shadow of a hope; it was not therefore a time at which it was most obvious to think of marriage. She conceived however that nothing should be omitted, which might alleviate, if it could not cure; and accordingly urged her speedy acceptance of the proposal. Fanny accordingly made the voyage to Lisbon; and the marriage took place on the twenty-fourth of February 1785.

The change of climate and situation was productive of little benefit; and the life of Fanny was only prolonged by a period of pregnancy, which soon declared itself. Mary, in the mean time, was impressed with the idea that her friend would die in this distant country; and, shocked with the recollection of her separation from the circle of her friends, determined to pass over to Lisbon to attend her. This resolution was treated by her acquaintance as in the utmost degree visionary; but she was not to be diverted from her point. She had not money to defray her expenses: she must quit for a long time the school, the very existence of which probably depended upon her exertions.

No person was ever better formed for the business of education; if it be not a sort of absurdity to speak of a person as formed for an inferior object, who is in possession of talents, in the fullest degree adequate to something on a more important and comprehensive scale. Mary had a quickness of temper, not apt to take offence with inadvertencies, but which led her to imagine that she saw the mind of the person with whom she had any transaction, and to refer the principle of her approbation or displeasure to the cordiality or injustice of their sentiments. She was occasionally severe and imperious in her resentments; and, when she strongly disapproved was apt to express her censure in terms that gave a very humiliating sensation to the person against whom it was directed. Her displeasure however never assumed its severest form, but when it was barbed by disappointment. Where she expected little, she was not very rigid in her censure of error.

But, to whatever the defects of her temper might amount, they were never exercised upon her inferiors in station or age. She scorned to make use of an ungenerous advantage, or to wound the defenceless. To her servants there never was a mistress more considerate or more kind. With children she was the mirror of patience. Perhaps, in all her extensive experience upon the subject of education, she never betrayed one symptom of irascibility. Her heart was the seat of every benevolent feeling; and accordingly, in all her intercourse with children, it was kindness and sympathy alone that prompted her conduct. Sympathy, when it mounts to a certain height, inevitably begets affection in the person towards whom it is exercised; and I have heard her say, that she never was concerned in the education of one child, who was not personally attached to her, and earnestly concerned not to incur her displeasure. Another eminent advantage she possessed in the business of education, was that she was little troubled with scepticism and uncertainty. She saw, as it were by intuition, the path which her mind determined to pursue, and had a firm confidence in her own power to effect what she desired. Yet, with all this, she had scarcely a tincture of obstinacy. She carefully watched symptoms as they rose, and the success of her experiments; and governed herself accordingly. While I thus enumerate her more than maternal qualities, it is impossible not to feel a pang at the recollection of her orphan children!

Though her friends earnestly dissuaded her from the journey to Lisbon, she found among them a willingness to facilitate the execution of her project, when it was once fixed. Mrs Burgh in particular, supplied her with money, which however she always conceived came from Dr Price. This loan, I have reason to believe, was faithfully repaid.

Her residence in Lisbon was not long. She arrived but a short time before her friend was prematurely delivered, and the event was fatal to both mother and child. Frances Blood, hitherto the chosen object of Mary's attachment, died on the twenty-ninth of November 1785.

It is thus that she speaks of her in her *Letters from Norway*, written ten years after her decease: 'When a warm heart has received strong impressions, they are not to be effaced. Emotions become sentiments; and the imagination renders even transient sensations permanent, by fondly retracing them. I cannot, without a thrill of delight, recollect views I have seen, which are not to be forgotten, nor looks I have felt in every nerve, which I shall never more meet. The grave has closed over a dear friend, the friend of my youth; still she is present with me, and I hear her soft voice warbling as I stray over the heath.'

CHAPTER FOUR

1785–1787

No doubt the voyage to Lisbon tended considerably to enlarge the understanding of Mary. She was admitted into the best company the English factory afforded. She made many profound observations on the character of the natives, and the baleful effect of superstition. The obsequies of Fanny, which it was necessary to perform by stealth and in darkness, tended to invigorate these observations in her mind.

She sailed upon her voyage home about the twentieth of December. On this occasion a circumstance occurred, that deserves to be recorded. While they were on their passage, they fell in with a French vessel, in great distress, and in daily expectation of foundering at sea, at the same time that it was almost destitute of provisions. The Frenchman hailed them, and intreated the English captain, in consideration of his melancholy situation, to take him and his crew on board. The Englishman represented in reply, that his stock of provisions was by no means adequate to such an additional number of mouths, and absolutely refused compliance. Mary, shocked at his apparent insensibility, took up the cause of the sufferers, and threatened the captain to have him called to a severe account, when he arrived in

England. She finally prevailed, and had the satisfaction to reflect, that the persons in question possibly owed their lives to her interposition.

When she arrived in England, she found that her school had suffered considerably in her absence. It can be little reproach to any one, to say that they were found incapable of supplying her place. She not only excelled in the management of the children, but had also the talent of being attentive and obliging to the parents, without degrading herself.

The period at which I am now arrived is important, as conducting to the first step of her literary career. Mr Hewlet had frequently mentioned literature to Mary as a certain source of pecuniary produce, and had urged her to make trial of the truth of his judgment. At this time she was desirous of assisting the father and mother of Fanny in an object they had in view, the transporting themselves to Ireland; and, as usual, what she desired in a pecuniary view, she was ready to take on herself to effect. For this purpose she wrote a duodecimo pamphlet of one hundred and sixty pages, entitled, *Thoughts on the Education of Daughters*. Mr Hewlet obtained from the bookseller, Mr Johnson in St Paul's Church Yard, ten guineas for the copyright of the manuscript, which she immediately applied to the object for the sake of which the pamphlet was written.

Every thing urged Mary to put an end to the affair of the school. She was dissatisfied with the different appearance it presented upon her return, from the state in which she left it. Experience impressed upon her a rooted aversion to that sort of cohabitation with her sisters, which the project of the school imposed. Cohabitation is a point of delicate experiment, and is, in a majority of instances, pregnant with ill-humour and unhappiness. The activity and ardent spirit of adventure which characterized Mary, were not felt in an equal degree by her sisters, so that a disproportionate share of every burthen attendant upon the situation, fell to her lot. On the other hand, they could scarcely perhaps be perfectly easy, in observing the superior degree of deference and courtship, which her merit extorted from almost every one that knew her. Her kindness for them was not diminished, but she resolved that the mode of its exertion in future should be different, tending to their benefit, without intrenching upon her own liberty.

Thus circumscribed, a proposal was made her, such as, regarding only the situations through which she had lately passed, is usually termed advantageous. This was, to accept the office of governess to the daughters of Lord Viscount Kingsborough, eldest son to the Earl of Kingston of the kingdom of Ireland. The terms held out to her were such as she determined to accept, at the same time resolving to retain the situation only for a short time. Independence was the object after which she thirsted, as she was fixed to try whether it might not be found in literary occupation. She was desirous however first to accumulate a small sum of money, which should enable her to consider at leisure the different literary engagements that might offer, and provide in some degree for the eventual deficiency of her earliest attempts.

The situation in the family of Lord Kingsborough, was offered to her through the medium of the Rev. Mr Prior, at that time one of the under masters of Eton school. She spent some time at the house of this gentleman, immediately after her giving up the school at Newington Green. Here she had an opportunity of making an accurate observation upon the manners and conduct of that celebrated seminary, and the ideas she retained of it were by no means favourable. By all that she saw, she was confirmed in a very favourite opinion of her's, in behalf of day-schools, where, as she expressed it, 'children have the opportunity of conversing with children, without interfering with domestic affections, the foundation of virtue.'

Though her residence in the family of Lord Kingsborough continued scarcely more than twelve months, she left behind her, with them and their connections, a very advantageous impression. The governesses the young ladies had hitherto had, were only a species of upper servants, controlled in every thing by the mother; Mary insisted upon the unbounded exercise of her own discretion. When the young ladies heard of their governess coming from England, they heard in imagination of a new enemy, and declared their resolution to guard themselves accordingly. Mary however speedily succeeded in gaining their confidence, and the friendship that soon grew up between her and Margaret King, now Countess Mount Cashel, the eldest daughter, was in an uncommon degree cordial and affectionate. Mary always spoke of this young lady in terms of the truest applause, both in relation to the eminence of her intellectual powers, and the ingenuous amiableness of her disposition. Lady Kingsborough, from the best motives, had imposed upon her daughters a variety of prohibitions, both as to the books they should read, and in many other respects. These prohibitions had their usual effects; inordinate desire for the things forbidden, and clandestine indulgence. Mary immediately restored the children to their liberty, and undertook to govern them by their affections only. The consequence was, that their indulgences were moderate, and they were uneasy under any indulgence that had not the sanction of their governess. The salutary effects of the new system of education were speedily visible; and Lady Kingsborough soon felt no other uneasiness, than lest the children should love their governess better than their mother.

Mary made many friends in Ireland, among the persons who visited Lord Kingsborough's house, for she always appeared there with the air of an equal, and not of a dependant. I have heard her mention the ludicrous distress of a woman of quality, whose name I have forgotten, that, in a large company, singled out Mary, and entered into a long conversation with her. After the conversation was over, she enquired whom she had been talking with, and found, to her utter mortification and dismay, that it was Miss King's governess.

One of the persons among her Irish acquaintance, whom Mary was accustomed to speak of with the highest respect, was Mr George Ogle, Member of Parliament for the county of Wexford. She held his talents in very high estimation; she was strongly prepossessed in favour of the goodness of his heart; and she always spoke of him as the most perfect gentleman she had ever known. She felt the regret of a disappointed friend, at the part he has lately taken in the politics of Ireland.

Lord Kingsborough's family passed the summer of the year 1787 at Bristol Hot-Wells, and had formed the project of proceeding from thence to the continent, a tour in which Mary purposed to accompany them. The plan however was ultimately given up, and Mary in consequence closed her connection with them, earlier than she otherwise had purposed to do.

At Bristol Hot-Wells she composed the little book which bears the title of *Mary, a Fiction*. A considerable part of this story consists, with certain modifications, of the incidents of her own friendship with Fanny. All the events that do not relate to that subject are fictitious.

This little work, if Mary had never produced any thing else, would serve, with persons of true taste and sensibility, to establish the eminence of her genius. The story is nothing. He that looks into the book only for incident, will probably lay it down with disgust. But the feelings are of the truest and most exquisite class; every circumstance is adorned with that species of imagination, which enlists itself under the banners of delicacy and sentiment. A work of sentiment, as it is called, is too often another name for a work of affectation. He that should imagine that the sentiments of this book are affected, would indeed be entitled to our profoundest commiseration.

CHAPTER FIVE

1787–1790

Being now determined to enter upon her literary plan, Mary came immediately from Bristol to the metropolis. Her conduct under this circumstance was such as to do credit both to her own heart, and that of Mr Johnson, her publisher, between whom and herself there now commenced an intimate friendship. She had seen him upon occasion of publishing her *Thoughts on the Education of Daughters*, and she addressed two or three letters to him during her residence in Ireland. Upon her arrival in London in August 1787, she went immediately to his house, and frankly explained to him her purpose, at the same time requesting his advice and assistance as to its execution. After a short conversation, Mr Johnson invited her to make his house her home, till she should have suited herself with a fixed residence. She accordingly resided at this time two or three weeks under his roof. At the same period she paid a visit or two of similar duration to some friends, at no great distance from the metropolis.

At Michaelmas 1787, she entered upon a house in George-street, on the Surrey side of Black Friar's Bridge, which Mr Johnson had provided for her during her excursion into the country. The three years immediately ensuing, may be said, in the ordinary acceptation of the term, to have been the most active period of her life. She brought with her to this habitation, the novel of *Mary*, which had not yet been sent to the press, and the commencement of the sort of oriental tale, entitled, *The Cave of Fancy*, which she thought proper afterwards to lay aside unfinished. I am told that at this period she appeared under great dejection of spirits, and filled with melancholy regret for the loss of her youthful friend. A period of two years had elapsed since the death of that friend; but it was possibly the composition of the fiction of *Mary*, that renewed her sorrows in their original force. Soon after entering upon her new habitation, she produced a little work, entitled, *Original Stories from Real Life*, intended for the use of children. At the commencement of her literary career, she is said to have conceived a vehement aversion to the being regarded, by her ordinary acquaintance, in the character of an author, and to have employed some precautions to prevent its occurrence.

The employment which the bookseller suggested to her, as the easiest and most certain source of pecuniary income, of course, was translation. With this view she improved herself in her French, with which she had previously but a slight acquaintance, and acquired the Italian and German languages. The greater part of her literary engagements at this time, were such as were presented to her by Mr Johnson. She new-modelled and abridged a work, translated from the Dutch, entitled, *Young Grandison*: she began a translation from the French, of a book, called, *The New Robinson*; but in this undertaking, she was, I believe, anticipated by another translator: and she compiled a series of extracts in verse and prose, upon the model of Dr Enfield's Speaker, which bears the title of *The Female Reader*; but which, from a cause not worth mentioning, has hitherto been printed with a different name in the title-page.

About the middle of the year 1788, Mr Johnson instituted the *Analytical Review*, in which Mary took a considerable share. She also translated Necker *On the Importance of Religious Opinions*; made an abridgment of Lavater's *Physiognomy*, from the French, which has never been published; and compressed Salzmann's *Elements of Morality*, a German production, into a publication in three volumes duodecimo. The translation of Salzmann produced a correspondence between Mary and the author; and he afterwards repaid the obligation to her in kind, by a German translation of *The Rights of Woman*. Such were her principal literary occupations, from the autumn of 1787, to the autumn of 1790.

It perhaps deserves to be remarked that this sort of miscellaneous literary employment, seems, for the time at least, rather to damp and contract, than to enlarge and invigorate, the genius. The writer is accustomed to see his performances answer the mere mercantile purpose of the day, and confounded with those of persons to whom he is secretly conscious of a superiority. No neighbour mind serves as a mirror to reflect the generous confidence he felt within himself; and perhaps the man never yet existed, who could maintain his enthusiasm to its full vigour, in the midst of this kind of solitariness. He is touched with the torpedo of mediocrity. I believe that nothing which Mary produced during this period, is marked with those daring flights, which exhibit themselves in the little fiction she composed just before its commencement. Among effusions of a nobler cast, I find occasionally interspersed some of that homily-language, which, to speak from my own feelings, is calculated to damp the moral courage it was intended to awaken. This is probably to be assigned to the causes above described.

I have already said that one of the purposes which Mary had conceived, a few years before, as necessary to give a relish to the otherwise insipid, or embittered, draught of human life, was usefulness. On this side, the period of her existence of which I am now treating, is more brilliant, than in a literary view. She determined to apply as great a part as possible of the produce of her present employments, to the assistance of her friends and of the distressed; and, for this purpose, laid down to herself rules of the most rigid economy. She began with endeavouring to promote the interest of her sisters. She conceived that there was no situation in which she could place them, at once so respectable and agreeable, as that of governesses in private families. She determined therefore in the first place, to endeavour to qualify them for such an undertaking. Her younger sister she sent to Paris, where she remained near two years. The elder she placed in a school near London, first as a parlour-boarder, and afterwards as a teacher. Her brother James, who had already been at sea, she first took into her house, and next sent to Woolwich for instruction, to qualify him for a respectable situation in the Royal Navy, where he was shortly after made a lieutenant. Charles, who was her favourite brother, had been articled to the eldest, an attorney in the Minories; but not being satisfied with his situation she removed him and in some time after, having first placed him with a farmer for instruction, she fitted him out for America, where his speculations, founded upon the basis she had provided, are said to have been extremely prosperous. The reason so much of this parental sort of care fell upon her was, that her father had by this time considerably embarrassed his circumstances. His affairs having grown too complex for himself to disentangle, he had entrusted them to the management of a near relation; but Mary, not being satisfied with the conduct of the business took them into her own hands. The exertions she made, and the struggle into which she entered however, in this instance, were ultimately fruitless. To the day of her death her father was almost wholly supported by funds which she supplied to him. In addition to her exertions for her own family, she took a young girl of about seven years of age under her protection and care, the niece of Mrs John Hunter, and of the present Mrs Skeys, for whose mother, then lately dead, she had entertained a sincere friendship.

The period, from the end of the year 1787 to the end of the year 1790, though consumed in labours of little eclat, served still further to establish her in a friendly connection from which she derived many pleasures. Mr Johnson, the bookseller, contracted a great personal regard for her, which resembled in many respects that of a parent. As she frequented his house, she of course became acquainted with his guests. Among these may be mentioned as persons possessing her esteem, Mr Bonnycastle, the mathematician, the late Mr George Anderson, accountant to the board of control, Dr George Fordyce, and Mr Fuseli, the celebrated painter. Between both of the two latter and herself, there existed sentiments of genuine affection and friendship.

CHAPTER SIX

1790–1792

Hitherto the literary career of Mary, had for the most part, been silent; and had been productive of income to herself, without apparently leading to the wreath of fame. From this time she was destined to attract the notice of the public, and perhaps no female writer ever obtained so great a degree of celebrity throughout Europe.

It cannot be doubted that, while, for three years of literary employment, she 'held the noiseless tenor of her way,' her mind was insensibly advancing towards a vigorous maturity. The uninterrupted habit of composition gave a freedom and firmness to the expression of her sentiments. The society she frequented, nourished her understanding, and enlarged her mind. The French revolution, while it gave a fundamental shock to the human intellect through every region of the globe, did not fail to produce a conspicuous effect in the progress of Mary's reflections. The prejudices of her early years suffered a vehement concussion. Her respect for establishments was undermined. At this period occurred a misunderstanding upon public grounds, with one of her early friends, whose attachment to musty creeds and exploded absurdities, had been increased, by the operation of those very circumstances, by which her mind had been rapidly advanced in the race of independence.

The event, immediately introductory to the rank which from this time she held in the lists of literature, was the publication of Burke's *Reflections on the Revolution in France*. This book, after having been long promised to the world, finally made its appearance on the first of November 1790; and Mary, full of sentiments of liberty, and impressed with a warm interest in the struggle that was now going on, seized her pen in the full burst of indignation, an emotion of which she was strongly susceptible. She was in the habit of composing with rapidity, and her answer, which was the first of the numerous ones that appeared, obtained extraordinary notice. Marked as it is with the vehemence and impetuousness of its eloquence, it is certainly chargeable with a too contemptuous and intemperate treatment of the great man against whom its attack is directed. But this circumstance was not injurious to the success of the publication. Burke had been warmly loved by the most liberal and enlightened friends of freedom, and they were proportionably inflamed and disgusted by the fury of his assault, upon what they deemed to be its sacred cause.

Short as was the time in which Mary composed her *Answer to Burke's Reflections*, there was one anecdote she told me concerning it, which seems worth recording in this place. It was sent to the press, as is the general practice when the early publication of a piece is deemed a matter of importance, before the composition was finished. When Mary had arrived at about the middle of her work, she was seized with a temporary fit of torpor and indolence, and began to repent of her undertaking. In this state of mind, she called, one evening, as she was in the practice of doing, upon her publisher, for the purpose of relieving herself by an hour or two's conversation. Here, the habitual ingenuousness of her nature, led her to describe what had just passed in her thoughts. Mr Johnson immediately, in a kind and friendly way, intreated her not to put any constraint upon her inclination, and to give herself no uneasiness about the sheets already printed, which he would cheerfully throw aside, if it would contribute to her happiness. Mary had wanted stimulus. She had not expected to be encouraged, in what she well knew to be an unreasonable access of idleness. Her friend's so readily falling in with her ill-humour, and seeming to expect that she would lay aside her undertaking, piqued her pride. She immediately went home; and proceeded to the end of her work, with no other interruptions but what were absolutely indispensable.

It is probable that the applause which attended her *Answer to Burke*, elevated the tone of her mind. She had always felt much confidence in her own powers; but it cannot be doubted, that the actual perception of a similar feeling respecting us in a multitude of others, must increase the confidence, and stimulate the adventure of any human being. Mary accordingly proceeded, in a short time after, to the composition of her most celebrated production, the *Vindication of the Rights of Woman*.

Never did any author enter into a cause, with a more ardent desire to be found, not a flourishing and empty declaimer, but an effectual champion. She considered herself as standing forth in defence of one half of the human species, labouring under a yoke which, through all the records of time, had degraded them from the station of rational beings, and almost sunk them to the level of the brutes. She saw indeed, that they were often attempted to be held in silken fetters, and bribed into the love of slavery; but the disguise and the treachery served only the more fully to confirm her opposition. She regarded her sex, in the language of Calista as

In every state of life the slaves of man:

the rich as alternately under the despotism of a father, a brother and a husband; and the middling and the poorer classes shut out from the acquisition of bread with independence, when they are not shut out from the very means of an industrious subsistence. Such were the views she entertained of the subject; and such were the feelings with which she warmed her mind.

The work is certainly a very bold and original production. The strength and firmness with which the author repels the opinions of Rousseau, Dr Gregory, and Dr James Fordyce, respecting the condition of women, cannot but make a strong impression upon every ingenuous reader. The public at large formed very different opinions respecting the character of the performance. Many of the sentiments are undoubtedly of a rather masculine description. The spirited and decisive way in which the author explodes the system of gallantry, and the species of homage with which the sex is usually treated, shocked the majority. Novelty produced a sentiment in their mind, which they mistook for a sense of injustice. The pretty, soft creatures that are so often to be found in the female sex, and that class of men who believe they could not exist without such pretty, soft creatures to resort to, were in arms against the author of so heretical and blasphemous a doctrine. There are also, it must be confessed, occasional passages of a stern and rugged feature, incompatible with the true stamina of the writer's character. But, if they did not belong to her fixed and permanent character, they belonged to her character *pro tempore*; and what she thought, she scorned to qualify.

Yet, along with this rigid, and somewhat amazonian temper, which characterized some parts of the book, it is impossible not to remark a luxuriance of imagination, and a trembling delicacy of sentiment, which would have done honour to a poet, bursting with all the visions of an Armida and a Dido.

The contradiction, to the public apprehension, was equally great, as to the person of the author, as it was when they considered the temper of the book. In the champion of her sex, who was described as endeavouring to invest them with all the rights of man, those whom curiosity prompted to seek the occasion of beholding her, expected to find a sturdy, muscular, raw-boned virago and they were not a little surprised, when, instead of all this, they found a woman, lovely in her person, and in the best and most engaging sense, feminine in her manners.

The *Vindication of the Rights of Woman* is undoubtedly a very unequal performance, and eminently deficient in method and arrangement. When tried by the hoary and long-established laws of literary composition, it can scarcely maintain its claim to be placed in the first class of human productions. But when we consider the importance of its doctrines, and the eminence of genius it displays, it seems not very improbable that it will be read as long as the English language endures. The publication of this book forms an epocha in the subject to which it belongs; and Mary Wollstonecraft will perhaps here-after be found to have performed more substantial service for the cause of her sex, than all the other writers, male or female, that ever felt themselves animated in the behalf of oppressed and injured beauty.

The censure of the liberal critic as to the defects of this performance, will be changed into astonishment, when I tell him, that a work of this inestimable moment, was begun, carried on, and finished in the state in which it now appears, in a period of no more than six weeks.

It is necessary here that I should resume the subject of the friendship that subsisted between Mary and Mr Fuseli, which proved the source of the most memorable events in her subsequent history. He is a native of the republic of Switzerland, but has spent the principal part of his life in the island of Great-Britain. The eminence of his genius can scarcely be disputed; it has indeed received the testimony which is the least to be suspected, that of some of the most considerable of his contemporary artists. He has one of the most striking characteristics of genius, a daring, as well as persevering, spirit of adventure. The work in which he is at present engaged, a series of pictures for the illustration of Milton, upon a very large scale, and produced solely upon the incitement of his own mind, is a proof of this, if indeed his whole life had not sufficiently proved it.

Mr Fuseli is one of Mr Johnson's oldest friends, and was at this time in the habit of visiting him two or three times a week. Mary, one of whose strongest characteristics was the exquisite sensations of pleasure she felt from the associations of visible objects, had hitherto never been acquainted, or never intimately acquainted, with an eminent painter. The being thus introduced therefore to the society of Mr Fuseli, was a high gratification to her; while he found in Mary, a person perhaps more susceptible of the emotions painting is calculated to excite, than any other with whom he ever conversed. Painting, and subjects closely connected with painting, were their almost constant topics of conversation; and they found them inexhaustible. It cannot be doubted, but that this was a species of exercise very conducive to the improvement of Mary's mind.

Nothing human however is unmixed. If Mary derived improvement from Mr Fuseli, she may also be suspected of having caught the infection of some of his faults. In early life Mr Fuseli was ardently attached to literature; but the demands of his profession have prevented him from keeping up that extensive and indiscriminate acquaintance with it, that belles-lettres scholars frequently possess. The favourites of his boyish years remain his only favourites. Homer is with Mr Fuseli the abstract and deposit of every human perfection. Milton, Shakespeare, and Richardson, have also engaged much of his attention. The nearest rival of Homer, I believe, if Homer can have a rival, is Jean-Jacques Rousseau. A young man embraces entire the opinions of a favourite writer, and Mr Fuseli has not had leisure to bring the opinions of his youth to a revision. Smitten with Rousseau's conception of the perfectness of the savage state, and the essential abortiveness of all civilization, Mr Fuseli looks at all our little attempts at improvement, with a spirit that borders perhaps too much upon contempt and indifference. One of his favourite positions is the divinity of genius. This is a power that comes complete at once from the hands of the Creator of all things, and the first essays of a man of real genius are such, in all their grand and most important features, as no subsequent assiduity can amend. Add to this, that Mr Fuseli is somewhat of a caustic turn of mind, with much wit, and a disposition to search, in every thing new or modern, for occasions of censure. I believe Mary came something more a cynic out of the school of Mr Fuseli, than she went into it.

But the principal circumstance that relates to the intercourse of Mary, and this celebrated artist, remains to be told. She saw Mr Fuseli frequently; he amused, delighted and instructed her. As a painter, it was impossible she should not wish to see his works, and consequently to frequent his house. She visited him; her visits were returned. Notwithstanding the inequality of their years, Mary was not of a temper to live upon terms of so much intimacy with a man of merit and genius, without loving him. The delight she enjoyed in his society, she transferred by association to his person. What she experienced in this respect, was no doubt heightened, by the state of celibacy and restraint in which she had hitherto lived, and to which the rules of polished society condemn an unmarried woman. She conceived a personal and ardent affection for him. Mr Fuseli was a married man, and his wife the acquaintance of Mary. She readily perceived the restrictions which this circumstance seemed to impose upon her; but she made light of any difficulty that might arise out of them. Not that she was insensible to the value of domestic endearments between persons of an opposite sex, but that she scorned to suppose, that she could feel a struggle, in conforming to the laws she should lay down to her conduct.

There cannot perhaps be a properer place than the present, to state her principles upon this subject, such at least as they were when I knew her best. She set a great value on a mutual affection between persons of an opposite sex. She regarded it as the principal solace of human life. It was her maxim, 'that the imagination should awaken the senses, and not the senses the imagination.' In other words, that whatever related to the gratification of the senses, ought to arise, in a human being of a pure mind, only as the consequence of an individual affection. She regarded the manners and habits of the majority of our sex in that respect, with strong disapprobation. She conceived that true virtue would prescribe the most entire celibacy, exclusively of affection, and the most perfect fidelity to that affection when it existed. There is no reason to doubt that, if Mr Fuseli had been disengaged at the period of their acquaintance, he would have been the man of her choice. As it was, she conceived it both practicable and eligible, to cultivate a distinguishing affection for him, and to foster it by the endearments of personal intercourse and a reciprocation of kindness, without departing in the smallest degree from the rules she prescribed to herself.

In September 1791, she removed from the house she occupied in George-street, to a large and commodious apartment in Store-street, Bedford-square. She began to think that she had been too rigid, in the laws of frugality and self-denial with which she set out in her literary career; and now added to the neatness and cleanliness which she had always scrupulously observed, a certain degree of elegance, and those temperate indulgences in furniture and accommodations, from which a sound and uncorrupted taste never fails to derive pleasure.

It was in the month of November in the same year (1791), that the writer of this narrative was first in company with the person to whom it relates. He dined with her at a friend's, together with Mr Thomas Paine and one or two other persons. The invitation was of his own seeking, his object being to see the author of *The Rights of Man*, with whom he had never before conversed.

The interview was not fortunate. Mary and myself parted, mutually displeased with each other. I had not read her *Rights of Woman*. I had barely looked into her *Answer to Burke*, and been displeased, as literary men are apt to be, with a few offences against grammar and other minute points of composition. I had therefore little curiosity to see Mrs Wollstonecraft, and a very great curiosity to see Thomas Paine. Paine, in his general habits, is no great talker; and, though he threw in occasionally some shrewd and striking remarks, the conversation lay principally between me and Mary. I, of consequence, heard her, very frequently when I wished to hear Paine.

We touched on a considerable variety of topics, and particularly on the characters and habits of certain eminent men. Mary, as has already been observed, had acquired in a very blameable degree, the practice of seeing every thing on the gloomy side, and bestowing censure with a plentiful hand, where circumstances were in any respect doubtful. I, on the contrary, had a strong propensity, to favourable construction, and particularly, where I found unequivocal marks of genius, strongly to incline to the supposition of generous and manly virtues. We ventilated in this way the characters of Voltaire and others, who have obtained from some individuals an ardent admiration, while the greater number have treated them with extreme moral severity. Mary was at last provoked to tell me, that praise, lavished in the way that I lavished it, could do no credit either to the commended or the commender. We discussed some questions on the subject of religion, in which her opinions approached much nearer to the received one, than mine. As the conversation proceeded, I became dissatisfied with the tone of my own share in it. We touched upon all topics, without treating forcibly and connectedly upon any. Meanwhile, I did her the justice, in giving an account of the conversation to a party in which I supped, though I was not sparing of my blame, to yield to her the praise of a person of active and independent thinking. On her side, she did me no part of what perhaps I considered as justice.

We met two or three times in the course of the following year, but made a very small degree of progress towards a cordial acquaintance.

In the close of the year 1792, Mary went over to France, where she continued to reside for upwards of two years. One of her principal inducements to this step, related, I believe, to Mr Fuseli. She had, at first, considered it as reasonable and judicious, to cultivate what I may be permitted to call, a Platonic affection for him; but she did not, in the sequel, find all the satisfaction in this plan, which she had originally expected from it. It was in vain that she enjoyed much pleasure in his society, and that she enjoyed it frequently. Her ardent imagination was continually conjuring up pictures of the happiness she should have found, if fortune had favoured their more intimate union. She felt herself formed for domestic affection, and all those tender charities, which men of sensibility have constantly treated as the dearest band of human society. General conversation and society could not satisfy her. She felt herself alone, as it were, in the great mass of her species; and she repined when she reflected, that the best years of her life were spent in this comfortless solitude. These ideas made the cordial intercourse of Mr Fuseli, which had at first been one of her greatest pleasures, a source of perpetual torment to her. She conceived it necessary to snap the chain of this association in her mind; and, for that purpose, determined to seek a new climate, and mingle in different scenes.

It is singular, that during her residence in Store-street, which lasted more than twelve months, she produced nothing, except a few articles in the *Analytical Review*. Her literary meditations were chiefly employed upon the sequel to *The Rights of Woman*; but she has scarcely left behind her a single paper, that can, with any certainty, be assigned to have had this destination.

CHAPTER SEVEN

1792–1795

The original plan of Mary, respecting her residence in France, had no precise limits in the article of duration; the single purpose she had in view being that of an endeavour to heal her distempered mind. She did not proceed so far as even to discharge her lodging in London; and, to some friends who saw her immediately before her departure, she spoke merely of an absence of six weeks.

It is not to be wondered at, that her excursion did not originally seem to produce the effects she had expected from it. She was in a land of strangers; she had no acquaintance; she had even to acquire the power of receiving and communicating ideas with facility in the language of the country. Her first residence was in a spacious mansion to which she had been invited, but the master of which (Monsieur Fillietaz) was absent at the time of her arrival. At first therefore she found herself surrounded only with servants. The gloominess of her mind communicated its own colour to the objects she saw; and in this temper she began a series of *Letters on the Present Character of the French Nation*, one of which she forwarded to her publisher, and which appears in the collection of her posthumous works. This performance she soon after discontinued; and it is, as she justly remarks, tinged with the saturnine temper which at that time pervaded her mind.

Mary carried with her introductions to several agreeable families in Paris. She renewed her acquaintance with Paine. There also subsisted a very sincere friendship between her and Helen Maria Williams, author of a collection of poems of uncommon merit, who at that time resided in Paris. Another person, whom Mary always spoke of in terms of ardent commendation, both for the excellence of his disposition and the force of his genius, was a Count Slabrendorf, by birth, I believe, a Swede. It is almost unnecessary to mention, that she was personally acquainted with the majority of the leaders in the French revolution.

But the house that, I believe, she principally frequented at this time, was that of Mr Thomas Christie, a person whose pursuits were mercantile, and who had written a volume on the French revolution. With Mrs Christie her acquaintance was more intimate than with her husband.

It was about four months after her arrival at Paris in December 1792, that she entered into that species of connection for which her heart secretly panted, and which had the effect of diffusing an immediate tranquillity and cheerfulness over her manners. The person with whom it was formed (for it would be an idle piece of delicacy to attempt to suppress a name, which is known to every one whom the reputation of Mary has reached), was Mr Gilbert Imlay, native of the United States of North America.

The place at which she first saw Mr Imlay was at the house of Mr Christie; and it perhaps deserves to be noticed, that the emotions he then excited in her mind, were, I am told, those of dislike, and that, for some time, she shunned all occasions of meeting him. This sentiment however speedily gave place to one of greater kindness.

Previously to the partiality she conceived for him, she had determined upon a journey to Switzerland, induced chiefly by motives of economy. But she had some difficulty in procuring a passport; and it was probably the intercourse that now originated between her and Mr Imlay, that changed her purpose, and led her to prefer a lodging at Neuilly, a village three miles from Paris. Her habitation here was a solitary house in the midst of a garden, with no other inhabitants than herself and the gardener, an old man, who performed for her many of the offices of a domestic, and would sometimes contend for the honour of making her bed. The gardener had a great veneration for his guest, and would set before her, when alone, some grapes of a particularly fine sort, which she could not without the greatest difficulty obtain when she had any person with her as a visitor. Here it was that she conceived, and for the most part executed, her *Historical and Moral View of the French Revolution*, into which, as she observes, are incorporated most of the observations she had collected for her *Letters*, and which was written with more sobriety and cheerfulness than the tone in which they had been commenced. In the evening she was accustomed to refresh herself by a walk in a neighbouring wood, from which her old host in vain endeavoured to dissuade her, by recounting divers horrible robberies and murders that had been committed there.

The commencement of the attachment Mary now formed, had neither confidant nor adviser. She always conceived it to be a gross breach of delicacy to have any confidant in a matter of this sacred nature, an affair of the heart. The origin of the connection was about the middle of April 1793, and it was carried on in a private manner for four months. At the expiration of that period a circumstance occurred that induced her to declare it. The French Convention, exasperated at the conduct of the British government, particularly in the affair of Toulon, formed a decree against the citizens of this country, by one article of which the English, resident in France, were ordered into prison till the period of a general peace. Mary had objected to a marriage with Mr Imlay, who, at the time their connection was formed, had no property whatever; because she would not involve him in certain family embarrassments to which she conceived herself exposed, or make him answerable for the pecuniary demands that existed against her. She however considered their engagement as of the most sacred nature; and they had mutually formed the plan of emigrating to America, as soon as they should have realized a sum, enabling them to do it in the mode they desired. The decree however that I have just mentioned, made it necessary, not that a marriage should actually take place, but that Mary should take the name of Imlay, which, from the nature of their connection, she conceived herself entitled to do, and obtain a certificate from the American ambassador, as the wife of a native of that country.

Their engagement being thus avowed, they thought proper to reside under the same roof, and for that purpose removed to Paris.

Mary was now arrived at the situation, which, for two or three preceding years, her reason had pointed out to her as affording the most substantial prospect of happiness. She had been tossed and agitated by the waves of misfortune. Her childhood, as she often said, had known few of the endearments, which constitute the principal happiness of childhood. The temper of her father had early given to her mind a severe cast of thought, and substituted the inflexibility of resistance for the confidence of affection. The cheerfulness of her entrance upon womanhood, had been darkened, by an attendance upon the deathbed of her mother, and the still more afflicting calamity of her eldest sister. Her exertions to create a joint independence for her sisters and herself, had been attended, neither with the success, nor the pleasure, she had hoped from them. Her first youthful passion, her friendship for Fanny, had encountered many disappointments, and, in fine, a melancholy and premature catastrophe. Soon after these accumulated mortifications, she was engaged in a contest with a near relation, whom she regarded as unprincipled, respecting the wreck of her father's fortune. In this affair she suffered the double pain, which arises from moral indignation, and disappointed benevolence. Her exertions to assist almost every member of her family, were great and unremitted. Finally, when she indulged a romantic affection for Mr Fuseli, and fondly imagined that she should find in it the solace of her cares, she perceived too late, that, by continually impressing on her mind fruitless images of unreserved affection and domestic felicity, it only served to give new pungency to the sensibility that was destroying her.

Some persons may be inclined to observe, that the evils here enumerated, are not among the heaviest in the catalogue of human calamities. But evils take their rank more from the temper of the mind that suffers them, than from their abstract nature. Upon a man of a hard and insensible disposition, the shafts of misfortune often fall pointless and impotent. There are persons, by no means hard and insensible, who, from an elastic and sanguine turn of mind, are continually prompted to look on the fair side of things, and, having suffered one fall, immediately rise again, to pursue their course, with the same eagerness, the same hope, and the same gaiety, as before. On the other hand, we not unfrequently meet with persons, endowed with the most exquisite and delicious sensibility, whose minds seem almost of too fine a texture to encounter the vicissitudes of human affairs, to whom pleasure is transport, and disappointment is agony indescribable. This character is finely portrayed by the author of *The Sorrows of Werter*. Mary was in this respect a female Werter.

She brought then, in the present instance, a wounded and sick heart, to take refuge in the bosom of a chosen friend. Let it not however be imagined, that she brought a heart, querulous, and ruined in its taste for pleasure. No; her whole character seemed to change with a change of fortune. Her sorrows, the depression of her spirits, were forgotten, and she assumed all the simplicity and the vivacity of a youthful mind. She was like a serpent upon a rock, that casts its slough, and appears again with the brilliancy, the sleekness, and the elastic activity of its happiest age. She was playful, full of confidence, kindness and sympathy. Her eyes assumed new lustre, and her cheeks new colour and smoothness. Her voice became cheerful; her temper overflowing with universal kindness; and that smile of bewitching tenderness from day to day illuminated her countenance, which all who knew her will so well recollect, and which won, both heart and soul, the affection of almost every one that beheld it.

Mary now reposed herself upon a person, of whose honour and principles she had the most exalted idea. She nourished an individual affection, which she saw no necessity of subjecting to restraint; and a heart like hers was not formed to nourish affection by halves. Her conception of Mr Imlay's 'tenderness and worth had twisted him closely round her heart;' and she 'indulged the thought, that she had thrown out some tendrils, to cling to the elm by which she wished to be supported.' This was 'talking a new language to her;' but 'conscious that she was not a parasite-plant,' she was willing to encourage and foster the luxuriances of affection. Her confidence was entire; her love was unbounded. Now, for the first time in her life, she gave a loose to all the sensibilities of her nature.

Soon after the time I am now speaking of, her attachment to Mr Imlay gained a new link, by finding reason to suppose herself with child.

Their establishment at Paris, was however broken up almost as soon as formed, by the circumstance of Mr Imlay's entering into business, urged, as he said, by the prospect of a family, and this being a favourable crisis in French affairs for commercial speculations. The pursuits in which he was engaged, led him in the month of September to Havre de Grace, then called Havre Marat, probably to superintend the shipping of goods, in which he was jointly engaged with some other person or persons. Mary remained in the capital.

The solitude in which she was now left, proved an unexpected trial. Domestic affections constituted the object upon which her heart was fixed; and she early felt, with an inward grief, that Mr Imlay 'did not attach those tender emotions round the idea of home, which, every time they recurred, dimmed her eyes with moisture.' She had expected his return from week to week, and from month to month; but a succession of business still continued to detain him at Havre. At the same time the sanguinary character which the government of France began every day to assume, contributed to banish tranquillity from the first months of her pregnancy. Before she left Neuilly, she happened one day to enter Paris on foot (I believe, by the *Place de Louis Quinze*), when an execution, attended with some peculiar aggravations, had just taken place, and the blood of the guillotine appeared fresh upon the pavement. The emotions of her soul burst forth in indignant exclamations, while a prudent bystander warned her of her danger, and intreated her to hasten and hide her discontents. She described to me, more than once, the anguish she felt at hearing of the death of Brissot, Vergniaud, and the twenty deputies, as one of the most intolerable sensations she had ever experienced.

Finding the return of Mr Imlay continually postponed, she determined, in January 1794, to join him at Havre. One motive that influenced her, though, I believe, by no means the principal, was the growing cruelties of Robespierre, and the desire she felt to be in any other place, rather than the devoted city; in the midst of which they were perpetrated.

From January to September, Mr Imlay and Mary lived together, with great harmony, at Havre, where the child, with which she was pregnant, was born, on the fourteenth of May, and named Frances, in remembrance of the dear friend of her youth, whose image could never be erased from her memory.

In September, Mr Imlay took his departure from Havre for the port of London. As this step was said to be necessary in the way of business, he endeavoured to prevail upon Mary to quit Havre, and once more take up her abode at Paris. Robespierre was now no more; and, of consequence, the only objection she had to residing in the capital, was removed. Mr Imlay was already in London, before she undertook her journey, and it proved the most fatiguing journey she ever made; the carriage, in which she travelled, being overturned no less than four times between Havre and Paris.

This absence, like that of the preceding year in which Mr Imlay had removed to Havre, was represented as an absence that was to have a short duration. In two months he was once again to join her in Paris. It proved however the prelude to an eternal separation. The agonies of such a separation, or rather desertion, great as Mary would have found them upon every supposition, were vastly increased, by the lingering method in which it was effected, and the ambiguity that, for a long time, hung upon it. This circumstance produced the effect, of holding her mind, by force, as it were, to the most painful of all subjects, and not suffering her to derive the just advantage from the energy and elasticity of her character.

The procrastination of which I am speaking was however productive of one advantage. It put off the evil day. She did not suspect the calamities that awaited her, till the close of the year. She gained an additional three months of comparative happiness. But she purchased it at a very dear rate. Perhaps no human creature ever suffered greater misery, than dyed the whole year 1795, in the life of this incomparable woman. It was wasted in that sort of despair, to the sense of which the mind is continually awakened, by a glimmering of fondly cherished, expiring hope.

Why did she thus obstinately cling to an ill-starred unhappy passion? Because it is of the very essence of affection, to seek to perpetuate itself. He does not love, who can resign this cherished sentiment, without suffering some of the sharpest struggles that our nature is capable of enduring. Add to this, Mary had fixed her heart upon this chosen friend; and one of the last impressions a worthy mind can submit to receive, is that of the worthlessness of the person upon whom it has fixed all its esteem. Mary had struggled to entertain a favourable opinion of human nature; she had unweariedly sought for a kindred mind, in whose integrity and fidelity to take up her rest. Mr Imlay undertook to prove, in his letters written immediately after their complete separation, that his conduct towards her was reconcilable to the strictest rectitude; but undoubtedly Mary was of a different opinion. Whatever the reader may decide in this respect, there is one sentiment that, I believe, he will unhesitatingly admit: that of pity for the mistake of the man, who, being in possession of such a friendship and attachment as those of Mary, could hold them at a trivial price, and, 'like the base Indian, throw a pearl away, richer than all his tribe.'

CHAPTER EIGHT

1795–1796

In April 1795, Mary returned once more to London, being requested to do so by Mr Imlay, who even sent a servant to Paris to wait upon her in the journey, before she could complete the necessary arrangements for her departure. But, notwithstanding these favourable appearances, she came to England with a heavy heart, not daring, after all the uncertainties and anguish she had endured, to trust to the suggestions of hope.

The gloomy forebodings of her mind, were but too faithfully verified. Mr Imlay had already formed another connection; as it is said, with a young actress from a strolling company of players. His attentions therefore to Mary were formal and constrained, and she probably had but little of his society. This alteration could not escape her penetrating glance. He ascribed it to pressure of business, and some pecuniary embarrassments which, at that time, occurred to him; it was of little consequence to Mary what was the cause. She saw, but too well, though she strove not to see, that his affections were lost to her for ever.

It is impossible to imagine a period of greater pain and mortification than Mary passed, for about seven weeks, from the sixteenth of April to the sixth of June, in a furnished house that Mr Imlay had provided for her. She had come over to England, a country for which she, at this time, expressed 'a repugnance, that almost amounted to horror,' in search of happiness. She feared that that happiness had altogether escaped her; but she was encouraged by the eagerness and impatience which Mr Imlay at length seemed to manifest for her arrival. When she saw him, all her fears were confirmed. What a picture was she capable of forming to herself, of the overflowing kindness of a meeting, after an interval of so much anguish and apprehension! A thousand images of this sort were present to her burning imagination. It is in vain, on such occasions, for reserve and reproach to endeavour to curb in the emotions of an affectionate heart. But the hopes she nourished were speedily blasted. Her reception by Mr Imlay was cold and embarrassed. Discussions ('explanations' they were called) followed; cruel explanations, that only added to the anguish of a heart already overwhelmed in grief! They had small pretensions indeed to explicitness; but they sufficiently told, that the case admitted not of remedy.

Mary was incapable of sustaining her equanimity in this pressing emergency. 'Love, dear, delusive love!' as she expressed herself to a friend some time afterwards, 'rigorous reason had forced her to resign; and now her rational prospects were blasted, just as she had learned to be contented with rational enjoyments.' Thus situated, life became an intolerable burthen. While she was absent from Mr Imlay, she could talk of purposes of separation and independence. But, now that they were in the same house, she could not withhold herself from endeavours to revive their mutual cordiality; and unsuccessful endeavours continually added fuel to the fire that destroyed her. She formed a desperate purpose to die.

This part of the story of Mary is involved in considerable obscurity. I only know, that Mr Imlay became acquainted with her purpose, at a moment when he was uncertain whether or not it were already executed, and that his feelings were roused by the intelligence. It was perhaps owing to his activity and representations, that her life, was, at this time, saved. She determined to continue to exist. Actuated by this purpose, she took a resolution, worthy both of the strength and affectionateness of her mind. Mr Imlay was involved in a question of considerable difficulty, respecting a mercantile adventure in Norway. It seemed to require the presence of some very judicious agent, to conduct the business to its desired termination. Mary determined to make the voyage, and take the business into her own hands. Such a voyage seemed the most desirable thing to recruit her health, and, if possible, her spirits, in the present crisis. It was also gratifying to her feelings, to be employed in promoting the interest of a man, from whom she had experienced such severe unkindness, but to whom she ardently desired to be reconciled. The moment of desperation I have mentioned, occurred in the close of May, and, in about a week after, she set out upon this new expedition.

The narrative of this voyage is before the world, and perhaps a book of travels that so irresistably seizes on the heart, never, in any other instance, found its way from the press. The occasional harshness and ruggedness of character, that diversify her *Vindication of the Rights of Woman*, here totally disappear. If ever there was a book calculated to make a man in love with its author, this appears to me to be the book. She speaks of her sorrows, in a way that fills us with melancholy, and dissolves us in tenderness, at the same time that she displays a genius which commands all our admiration. Affliction had tempered her heart to a softness almost more than human; and the gentleness of her spirit seems precisely to accord with all the romance of unbounded attachment.

Thus softened and improved, thus fraught with imagination and sensibility, with all, and more than all, 'that youthful poets fancy, when they love,' she returned to England, and, if he had so pleased, to the arms of her lover. Her return was hastened by the ambiguity, to her apprehension, of Mr Imlay's conduct. He had promised to meet her upon her return from Norway, probably at Hamburg; and they were then to pass some time in Switzerland. The style however of his letters to her during her tour, was not such as to inspire confidence; and she wrote to him very urgently, to explain himself, relative to the footing upon which they were hereafter to stand to each other. In his answer, which reached her at Hamburg, he treated her questions as 'extraordinary and unnecessary,' and desired her to be at the pains to decide for herself. Feeling herself unable to accept this as an explanation, she instantly determined to sail for London by the very first opportunity, that she might thus bring to a termination the suspense that preyed upon her soul.

It was not long after her arrival in London in the commencement of October, that she attained the certainty she sought. Mr Imlay procured her a lodging. But the neglect she experienced from him after she entered it, flashed conviction upon her, in spite of his asseverations. She made further enquiries, and at length was informed by a servant, of the real state of the case. Under the immediate shock which the painful certainty gave her, her first impression was to repair to him at the ready-furnished house he had provided for his new mistress. What was the particular nature of their conference I am unable to relate. It is sufficient to say that the wretchedness of the night which succeeded this fatal discovery, impressed her with the feeling, that she would sooner suffer a thousand deaths, than pass another of equal misery.

The agony of her mind determined her; and that determination gave her a sort of desperate serenity. She resolved to plunge herself in the Thames; and, not being satisfied with any spot nearer to London, she took a boat, and rowed to Putney. Her first thought had led her to Battersea-bridge, but she found it too public. It was night when she arrived at Putney, and by that time it had begun to rain with great violence. The rain suggested to her the idea of walking up and down the bridge, till her clothes were thoroughly drenched and heavy with the wet, which she did for half an hour without meeting a human being. She then leaped from the top of the bridge, but still seemed to find a difficulty in sinking, which she endeavoured to counteract by pressing her clothes closely round her. After some time she became insensible; but she always spoke of the pain she underwent as such, that, though she could afterwards have determined upon almost any other species of voluntary death, it would have been impossible for her to resolve upon encountering the same sensations again. I am doubtful, whether this is to be ascribed to the mere nature of suffocation, or was not rather owing to the preternatural action of a desperate spirit.

After having been for a considerable time insensible, she was recovered by the exertions of those by whom the body was found. She had sought, with cool and deliberate firmness, to put a period to her existence, and yet she lived to have every prospect of a long possession of enjoyment and happiness. It is perhaps not an unfrequent case with suicides, that we find reason to suppose, if they had survived their gloomy purpose, that they would, at a subsequent period, have been considerably happy. It arises indeed, in some measure, out of the very nature of a spirit of self-destruction; which implies a degree of anguish, that the constitution of the human mind will not suffer to remain long undiminished. This is a serious reflection. Probably no man would destroy himself from an impatience of present pain, if he felt a moral certainty that there were years of enjoyment still in reserve for him. It is perhaps a futile attempt, to think of reasoning with a man in that state of mind which precedes suicide. Moral reasoning is nothing but the awakening of certain feelings; and the feeling by which he is actuated, is too strong to leave us much chance of impressing him with other feelings, that should have force enough to counter-balance it. But, if the prospect of future tranquillity and pleasure cannot be expected to have much weight with a man under an immediate purpose of suicide, it is so much the more to be wished, that men would impress their minds, in their sober moments, with a conception, which, being rendered habitual, seems to promise to act as a successful antidote in a paroxysm of desperation.

The present situation of Mary, of necessity produced some further intercourse between her and Mr Imlay. He sent a physician to her; and Mrs Christie, at his desire, prevailed on her to remove to her house in Finsbury-square. In the mean time Mr Imlay assured her that his present was merely a casual sensual connection; and, of course, fostered in her mind the idea that it would be once more in her choice to live with him. With whatever intention the idea was suggested, it was certainly calculated to increase the agitation of her mind. In one respect however it produced an effect unlike that which might most obviously have been looked for. It roused within her the characteristic energy of mind, which she seemed partially to have forgotten. She saw the necessity of bringing the affair to a point, and not suffering months and years to roll on in uncertainty and suspense. This idea inspired her with an extraordinary resolution. The language she employed, was, in effect, as follows: 'If we are ever to live together again, it must be now. We meet now, or we part for ever. You say, you cannot abruptly break off the connection you have formed. It is unworthy of my courage and character, to wait the uncertain issue of that connection. I am determined to come to a decision. I consent then, for the present, to live with you, and the woman to whom you have associated yourself. I think it important that you should learn habitually to feel for your child the affection of a father. But, if you reject this proposal, here we end. You are now free. We will correspond no more. We will have no intercourse of any kind. I will be to you as a person that is dead.'

The proposal she made, extraordinary and injudicious as it was, was at first accepted; and Mr Imlay took her accordingly, to look at a house he was upon the point of hiring, that she might judge whether it was calculated to please her. Upon second thoughts however he retracted his concession.

In the following month, Mr Imlay, and the woman with whom he was at present connected, went to Paris, where they remained three months. Mary had, previously to this, fixed herself in a lodging in Finsbury-place, where, for some time, she saw scarcely any one but Mrs Christie, for the sake of whose neighbourhood she had chosen this situation; 'existing,' as she expressed it, 'in a living tomb, and her life but an exercise of fortitude, continually on the stretch.'

Thus circumstanced, it was unavoidable for her thoughts to brood upon a passion, which all that she had suffered had not yet been able to extinguish. Accordingly, as soon as Mr Imlay returned to England, she could not restrain herself from making another effort, and desiring to see him once more. 'During his absence, affection had led her to make numberless excuses for his conduct,' and she probably wished to believe that his present connection was, as he represented it, purely of a casual nature. To this application, she observes, that 'he returned no other answer, except declaring, with unjustifiable passion, that he would not see her.'

This answer, though, at the moment, highly irritating to Mary, was not the ultimate end of the affair. Mr Christie was connected in business with Mr Imlay, at the same time that the house of Mr Christie was the only one at which Mary habitually visited. The consequence of this was, that, when Mr Imlay had been already more than a fortnight in town, Mary called at Mr Christie's one evening, at a time when Mr Imlay was in the parlour. The room was full of company. Mrs Christie heard Mary's voice in the passage, and hastened to her, to intreat her not to make her appearance. Mary however was not to be controlled. She thought, as she afterwards told me, that it was not consistent with conscious rectitude, that she should shrink, as if abashed, from the presence of one by whom she deemed herself injured. Her child was with her. She entered; and, in a firm manner, immediately led up the child, now near two years of age, to the knees of its father. He retired with Mary into another apartment, and promised to dine with her at her lodging, I believe, the next day.

In the interview which took place in consequence of this appointment, he expressed himself to her in friendly terms, and in a manner calculated to soothe her despair. Though he could conduct himself, when absent from her, in a way which she censured as unfeeling; this species of sternness constantly expired when he came into her presence. Mary was prepared at this moment to catch at every phantom of happiness; and the gentleness of his carriage, was to her as a sunbeam, awakening the hope of returning day. For an instant she gave herself up to delusive visions; and, even after the period of delirium expired, she still dwelt, with an aching eye, upon the air-built and unsubstantial prospect of a reconciliation.

At his particular request, she retained the name of Imlay, which, a short time before, he had seemed to dispute with her. 'It was not,' as she expresses herself in a letter to a friend, 'for the world that she did so – not in the least – but she was unwilling to cut the Gordian knot, or tear herself away in appearance, when she could not in reality.'

The day after this interview, she set out upon a visit to the country, where she spent nearly the whole of the month of March. It was, I believe, while she was upon this visit, that some epistolary communication with Mr Imlay, induced her resolutely to expel from her mind, all remaining doubt as to the issue of the affair.

Mary was now aware that every demand of forbearance towards him, of duty to her child, and even of indulgence to her own deep-rooted predilection, was discharged. She determined to rouse herself, and cast off for ever an attachment, which to her had been a spring of inexhaustible bitterness. Her present residence among the scenes of nature, was favourable to this purpose. She was at the house of an old and intimate friend, a lady of the name of Cotton, whose partiality for her was strong and sincere. Mrs Cotton's nearest neighbour was Sir William East, baronet; and, from the joint effect of the kindness of her friend, and the hospitable and distinguishing attentions of this respectable family, she derived considerable benefit. She had been amused and interested in her journey to Norway; but with this difference, that, at that time, her mind perpetually returned with trembling anxiety to conjectures respecting Mr Imlay's future conduct, whereas now, with a lofty and undaunted spirit, she threw aside every thought that recurred to him, while she felt herself called upon to make one more effort for life and happiness.

Once after this, to my knowledge, she saw Mr Imlay; probably, not long after her return to town. They met by accident upon the New Road; he alighted from his horse, and walked with her for some time; and the rencounter passed, as she assured me, without producing in her any oppressive emotion.

Be it observed, by the way, and I may be supposed best to have known the real state of the case, she never spoke of Mr

Imlay with acrimony, and was displeased when any person, in her hearing, expressed contempt of him. She was characterized by a strong sense of indignation; but her emotions of this sort, were short-lived, and in no long time subsided into a dignified sereneness and equanimity.

The question of her connection with Mr Imlay, as we have seen, was not completely dismissed, till March 1796. But it is worthy to be observed, that she did not, like ordinary persons under extreme anguish of mind, suffer her understanding, in the mean time, to sink into littleness and debility. The most inapprehensive reader may conceive what was the mental torture she endured, when he considers, that she was twice, with an interval of four months, from the end of May to the beginning of October, prompted by it to purposes of suicide. Yet in this period she wrote her *Letters from Norway*. Shortly after its expiration she prepared them for the press, and they were published in the close of that year. In January 1796, she finished the sketch of a comedy, which turns, in the serious scenes, upon the incidents of her own story. It was offered to both the winter-managers, and remained among her papers at the period of her decease; but it appeared to me to be in so crude and imperfect a state, that I judged it most respectful to her memory to commit it to the flames. To understand this extraordinary degree of activity, we must recollect however the entire solitude, in which most of her hours at that time were consumed.

CHAPTER NINE

1796–1797

I am now led, by the progress of the story, to the last branch of her history, the connection between Mary and myself. And this I shall relate with the same simplicity that has pervaded every other part of my narrative. If there ever were any motives of prudence or delicacy, that could impose a qualification upon the story, they are now over. They could have no relation but to factitious rules of decorum. There are no circumstances of her life, that, in the judgment of honour and reason, could brand her with disgrace. Never did there exist a human being, that needed, with less fear, expose all their actions, and call upon the universe to judge them. An event of the most deplorable sort, has awfully imposed silence upon the gabble of frivolity.

We renewed our acquaintance in January 1796, but with no particular effect, except so far as sympathy in her anguish, added in my mind to the respect I had always entertained for her talents. It was in the close of that month that I read her *Letters from Norway*; and the impression that book produced upon me has been already related.

It was on the fourteenth of April that I first saw her after her excursion into Berkshire. On that day she called upon me in

Somers Town, she having, since her return, taken a lodging in Cumming-street, Pentonville, at no great distance from the place of my habitation. From that time our intimacy increased, by regular, but almost imperceptible degrees.

The partiality we conceived for each other, was in that mode, which I have always regarded as the purest and most refined style of love. It grew with equal advances in the mind of each. It would have been impossible for the most minute observer to have said who was before, and who was after. One sex did not take the priority which long-established custom has awarded it, nor the other overstep that delicacy which is so severely imposed. I am not conscious that either party can assume to have been the agent or the patient, the toil-spreader or the prey, in the affair. When, in the course of things, the disclosure came, there was nothing, in a manner, for either party to disclose to the other.

In July 1796 I made an excursion into the county of Norfolk, which occupied nearly the whole of that month. During this period Mary removed, from Cumming-street, Pentonville, to Judd-place West, which may be considered as the extremity of Somers Town. In the former situation, she had occupied a furnished lodging. She had meditated a tour to Italy or Switzerland, and knew not how soon she should set out with that view. Now however she felt herself reconciled to a longer abode in England, probably without exactly knowing why this change had taken place in her mind. She had a quantity of furniture locked up at a broker's ever since her residence in Store-street, and she now found it advisable to bring it into use. This circumstance occasioned her present removal.

The temporary separation attendant on my little journey, had its effect on the mind of both parties. It gave a space for the maturing of inclination. I believe that, during this interval, each furnished to the other the principal topic of solitary and daily contemplation. Absence bestows a refined and aerial delicacy upon affection, which it with difficulty acquires in any other way. It seems to resemble the communication of spirits, without the medium, or the impediment, of this earthly frame.

When we met again, we met with new pleasure, and, I may add, with a more decisive preference for each other. It was how-ever three weeks longer, before the sentiment which trembled upon the tongue, burst from the lips of either. There was, as I have already said, no period of throes and resolute explana-tion attendant on the tale. It was friendship melting into love. Previously to our mutual declaration, each felt half-assured, yet each felt a certain trembling anxiety to have assurance complete.

Mary rested her head upon the shoulder of her lover, hoping to find a heart with which she might safely treasure her world of affection; fearing to commit a mistake, yet, in spite of her melancholy experience, fraught with that generous confidence, which, in a great soul, is never extinguished. I had never loved till now; or, at least, had never nourished a passion to the same growth, or met with an object so consummately worthy.

We did not marry. It is difficult to recommend any thing to indiscriminate adoption, contrary to the established rules and prejudices of mankind; but certainly nothing can be so ridiculous upon the face of it, or so contrary to the genuine march of sentiment, as to require the overflowing of the soul to wait upon a ceremony, and that at which, wherever delicacy and imagination exist, is of all things most sacredly private, to blow a trumpet before it, and to record the moment when it has arrived at its climax.

There were however other reasons why we did not immediately marry. Mary felt an entire conviction of the propriety of her conduct. It would be absurd to suppose that, with a heart withered by desertion, she was not right to give way to the emotions of kindness which our intimacy produced, and to seek for that support in friendship and affection, which could alone give pleasure to her heart, and peace to her meditations. It was only about six months since she had resolutely banished every thought of Mr Imlay; but it was at least eighteen that he ought to have been banished, and would have been banished, had it not been for her scrupulous pertinacity in determining to leave no measure untried to regain him. Add to this, that the laws of etiquette ordinarily laid down in these cases, are essentially absurd, and that the sentiments of the heart cannot submit to be directed by the rule and square. But Mary had an extreme aversion to be made the topic of vulgar discussion; and, if there be any weakness in this, the dreadful trials through which she had recently passed, may well plead in its excuse. She felt that she had been too much, and too rudely spoken of, in the former instance; and she could not resolve to do any thing that should immediately revive that painful topic.

For myself, it is certain that I had for many years regarded marriage with so well-grounded an apprehension, that, notwithstanding the partiality for Mary that had taken possession of my soul, I should have felt it very difficult, at least in the present stage of our intercourse, to have resolved on such a measure. Thus, partly from similar, and partly from different motives, we felt alike in this, as we did perhaps in every other circumstance that related to our intercourse.

I have nothing further that I find it necessary to record, till the commencement of April 1797. We then judged it proper to declare our marriage, which had taken place a little before. The principal motive for complying with this ceremony, was the circumstance of Mary being in a state of pregnancy. She was unwilling, and perhaps with reason, to incur that exclusion from the society of many valuable and excellent individuals, which custom awards in cases of this sort. I should have felt an extreme repugnance to the having caused her such an inconvenience. And, after the experiment of seven months of as intimate an intercourse as our respective modes of living would admit, there was certainly less hazard to either, in the subjecting ourselves to those consequences which the laws of England annex to the relations of husband and wife. On the sixth of April we entered into possession of a house, which had been taken by us in concert.

In this place I have a very curious circumstance to notice, which I am happy to have occasion to mention, as it tends to expose certain regulations of polished society, of which the absurdity vies with the odiousness. Mary had long possessed the advantage of an acquaintance with many persons of genius, and with others whom the effects of an intercourse with elegant society, combined with a certain portion of information and good sense, sufficed to render amusing companions. She had lately extended the circle of her acquaintance in this respect;

and her mind, trembling between the opposite impressions of past anguish and renovating tranquillity, found ease in this species of recreation. Wherever Mary appeared, admiration attended upon her. She had always displayed talents for conversation; but maturity of understanding, her travels, her long residence in France, the discipline of affliction, and the smiling, new-born peace which awaked a corresponding smile in her animated countenance, inexpressibly increased them. The way in which the story of Mr Imlay was treated in these polite circles, was probably the result of the partiality she excited. These elegant personages were divided between their cautious adherence to forms, and the desire to seek their own gratification. Mary made no secret of the nature of her connection with Mr Imlay; and in one instance, I well know, she put herself to the trouble of explaining it to a person totally indifferent to her, because he never failed to publish every thing he knew, and, she was sure, would repeat her explanation to his numerous acquaintance. She was of too proud and generous a spirit to stoop to hypocrisy. These persons however, in spite of all that could be said, persisted in shutting their eyes, and pretending they took her for a married woman.

Observe the consequence of this! While she was, and constantly professed to be, an unmarried mother; she was fit society for the squeamish and the formal. The moment she acknowledged herself a wife, and that by a marriage perhaps unexceptionable, the case was altered. Mary and myself, ignorant as we were of these elevated refinements, supposed that our marriage would place her upon a surer footing in the calendar of polished society, than ever. But it forced these people to see the truth, and to confess their belief of what they had carefully been told; and this they could not forgive. Be it remarked, that the date of our marriage had nothing to do with this, that question being never once mentioned during this period. Mary indeed had, till now, retained the name of Imlay which had first been assumed from necessity in France; but its being retained thus long, was purely from the awkwardness that attends the introduction of a change, and not from an apprehension of consequences of this sort. Her scrupulous explicitness as to the nature of her situation, surely sufficed to make the name she bore perfectly immaterial.

It is impossible to relate the particulars of such a story, but in the language of contempt and ridicule. A serious reflection however upon the whole, ought to awaken emotions of a different sort. Mary retained the most numerous portion of her acquaintance, and the majority of those whom she principally valued. It was only the supporters and the subjects of the unprincipled manners of a court, that she lost. This however is immaterial. The tendency of the proceeding, strictly considered, and uniformly acted upon, would have been to proscribe her from all valuable society. And who was the person proscribed? The firmest champion, and, as I strongly suspect, the greatest ornament her sex ever had to boast! A woman, with sentiments as pure, as refined, and as delicate, as ever inhabited a human heart! It is fit that such persons should stand by, that we may have room enough for the dull and insolent dictators, the gamblers, and demireps of polished society.

Two of the persons, the loss of whose acquaintance Mary principally regretted upon this occasion, were Mrs Inchbald and Mrs Siddons. Their acquaintance, it is perhaps fair to observe, is to be ranked among her recent acquisitions. Mrs Siddons, I am sure, regretted the necessity, which she conceived to be imposed on her by the peculiarity of her situation, to conform to the rules I have described. She is endowed with that rich and generous sensibility, which should best enable its possessor completely to feel the merits of her deceased friend. She very truly observes, in a letter now before me, that the *Travels in Norway* were read by no one, who was in possession of 'more reciprocity of feeling, or more deeply impressed with admiration of the writer's extraordinary powers.'

Mary felt a transitory pang, when the conviction reached her of so unexpected a circumstance, that was rather exquisite. But she disdained to sink under the injustice (as this ultimately was) of the supercilious and the foolish, and presently shook off the impression of the first surprize. That once subsided, I well knew that the event was thought of, with no emotions, but those of superiority to the injustice she sustained; and was not of force enough to diminish a happiness, which seemed hourly to become more vigorous and firm.

I think I may venture to say, that no two persons ever found in each other's society, a satisfaction more pure and refined. What it was in itself, can now only be known, in its full extent, to the survivor. But, I believe, the serenity of her countenance, the increasing sweetness of her manners, and that consciousness of enjoyment that seemed ambitious that every one she saw should be happy as well as herself, were matters of general observation to all her acquaintance. She had always possessed, in an unparalleled degree, the art of communicating happiness, and she was now in the constant and unlimited exercise of it.

She seemed to have attained that situation, which her disposition and character imperiously demanded, but which she had never before attained; and her understanding and her heart felt the benefit of it.

While we lived as near neighbours only, and before our last removal, her mind had attained considerable tranquillity, and was visited but seldom with those emotions of anguish, which had been but too familiar to her. But the improvement in this respect, which accrued upon our removal and establishment, was extremely obvious. She was a worshipper of domestic life. She loved to observe the growth of affection between me and her daughter, then three years of age, as well as my anxiety respecting the child not yet born. Pregnancy itself, unequal as the decree of nature seems to be in this respect, is the source of a thousand endearments. No one knew better than Mary how to extract sentiments of exquisite delight, from trifles, which a suspicious and formal wisdom would scarcely deign to remark. A little ride into the country with myself and the child, has sometimes produced a sort of opening of the heart, a general expression of confidence and affectionate soul, a sort of infantile, yet dignified endearment, which those who have felt may understand, but which I should in vain attempt to portray.

In addition to our domestic pleasures, I was fortunate enough to introduce her to some of my acquaintance of both sexes, to whom she attached herself with all the ardour of approbation and friendship.

Ours was not an idle happiness, a paradise of selfish and transitory pleasures. It is perhaps scarcely necessary to mention, that, influenced by the ideas I had long entertained upon the subject of cohabitation, I engaged an apartment, about twenty doors from our house in the Polygon, Somers Town, which I designed for the purpose of my study and literary occupations. Trifles however will be interesting to some readers, when they relate to the last period of the life of such a person as Mary. I will add therefore, that we were both of us of opinion, that it was possible for two persons to be too uniformly in each other's society. Influenced by that opinion, it was my practice to repair to the apartment I have mentioned as soon as I rose, and frequently not to make my appearance in the Polygon, till the hour of dinner. We agreed in condemning the notion, prevalent in many situations in life, that a man and his wife cannot visit in mixed society, but in company with each other; and we rather sought occasions of deviating from, than of complying with, this rule. By these means, though, for the most part, we spent the latter half of each day in one another's society, yet we were in no danger of satiety. We seemed to combine, in a considerable degree, the novelty and lively sensation of a visit, with the more delicious and heart-felt pleasures of domestic life.

Whatever may be thought, in other respects, of the plan we laid down to ourselves, we probably derived a real advantage from it, as to the constancy and uninterruptedness of our literary pursuits. Mary had a variety of projects of this sort, for the exercise of her talents, and the benefit of society; and, if she had lived, I believe the world would have had very little reason to complain of any remission of her industry. One of her projects, which has been already mentioned, was of a series of *Letters on the Management of Infants*. Though she had been for some time digesting her views on this subject with a view to the press, I have found comparatively nothing that she had committed to paper respecting it. Another project, of longer standing, was of a series of books for the instruction of children. A fragment she left in execution of this project, is inserted in her *Posthumous Works*.

But the principal work, in which she was engaged for more than twelve months before her decease, was a novel, entitled, *The Wrongs of Woman*. I shall not stop here to explain the nature of the work, as so much of it as was already written, is now given to the public. I shall only observe that, impressed, as she could not fail to be, with the consciousness of her talents, she was desirous, in this instance, that they should effect what they were capable of effecting. She was sensible how arduous a task it is to produce a truly excellent novel; and she roused her faculties to grapple with it. All her other works were produced with a rapidity, that did not give her powers time fully to expand. But this was written slowly and with mature considerations. She began it in several forms, which she successively rejected, after they were considerably advanced. She wrote many parts of the work again and again, and, when she had finished what she intended for the first part, she felt herself more urgently stimulated to revise and improve what she had written, than to proceed, with constancy of application, in the parts that were to follow.

CHAPTER TEN

I am now led, by the course of my narrative, to the last fatal scene of her life. She was taken in labour on Wednesday, the thirtieth of August. She had been somewhat indisposed on the preceding Friday, the consequence, I believe, of a sudden alarm. But from that time she was in perfect health. She was so far from being under any apprehension as to the difficulties of child-birth, as frequently to ridicule the fashion of ladies in England, who keep their chamber for one full month after delivery. For herself, she proposed coming down to dinner on the day immediately following. She had already had some experience on the subject in the case of Fanny; and I cheerfully submitted in every point to her judgment and her wisdom. She hired no nurse. Influenced by ideas of decorum, which certainly ought to have no place, at least in cases of danger, she determined to have a woman to attend her in the capacity of midwife. She was sensible that the proper business of a midwife, in the instance of a natural labour, is to sit by and wait for the operations of nature, which seldom, in these affairs, demand the interposition of art.

At five o'clock in the morning of the day of delivery, she felt what she conceived to be some notices of the approaching labour. Mrs Blenkinsop, matron and midwife to the Westminster Lying-in Hospital, who had seen Mary several times previous to her delivery, was soon after sent for, and arrived about nine. During the whole day Mary was perfectly cheerful. Her pains came on slowly; and, in the morning, she wrote several notes, three addressed to me, who had gone, as usual, to my apartments, for the purpose of study. About two o'clock in the afternoon, she went up to her chamber, – never more to descend.

The child was born at twenty minutes after eleven at night. Mary had requested that I would not come into the chamber till all was over, and signified her intention of then performing the interesting office of presenting the new-born child to its father. I was sitting in a parlour; and it was not till after two o'clock on Thursday morning, that I received the alarming intelligence, that the placenta was not yet removed, and that the midwife dared not proceed any further, and gave her opinion for calling in a male practitioner. I accordingly went for Dr Poignand, physician and man-midwife to the same hospital, who arrived between three and four hours after the birth of the child. He immediately proceeded to the extraction of the placenta, which he brought away in pieces, till he was satisfied that the whole was removed. In that point however it afterwards appeared that he was mistaken.

The period from the birth of the child till about eight o'clock the next morning, was a period full of peril and alarm. The loss of blood was considerable, and produced an almost uninterrupted series of fainting fits. I went to the chamber soon after four in the morning, and found her in this state. She told me some time on Thursday, 'that she should have died the preceding night, but that she was determined not to leave me.' She added, with one of those smiles which so eminently illuminated her countenance, 'that I should not be like Porson,' alluding to the circumstance of that great man having lost his wife, after being only a few months married. Speaking of what she had already passed through, she declared, 'that she had never known what bodily pain was before.'

On Thursday morning Dr Poignand repeated his visit. Mary had just before expressed some inclination to see Dr George Fordyce, a man probably of more science than any other medical professor in England, and between whom and herself there had long subsisted a mutual friendship. I mentioned this to Dr Poignand, but he rather discountenanced the idea, observing that he saw no necessity for it, and that he supposed Dr Fordyce was not particularly conversant with obstetrical cases; but that I would do as I pleased. After Dr Poignand was gone, I determined to send for Dr Fordyce. He accordingly saw the patient about three o'clock on Thursday afternoon. He however perceived no particular cause of alarm; and, on that or the next day, quoted, as I am told, Mary's case, in a mixed company, as a corroboration of a favourite idea of his, of the propriety of employing females in the capacity of midwives. Mary 'had had a woman, and was doing extremely well.'

What had passed however in the night between Wednesday and Thursday, had so far alarmed me, that I did not quit the house, and scarcely the chamber, during the following day. But my alarms wore off, as time advanced. Appearances were more favourable, than the exhausted state of the patient would almost have permitted me to expect. Friday morning therefore I devoted to a business of some urgency, which called me to different parts of the town, and which, before dinner, I happily completed. On my return, and during the evening, I received the most pleasurable sensations from the promising state of the patient. I was now perfectly satisfied that every thing was safe, and that, if she did not take cold, or suffer from any external accident, her speedy recovery was certain.

Saturday was a day less auspicious than Friday, but not absolutely alarming.

Sunday, the third of September, I now regard as the day, that finally decided on the fate of the object dearest to my heart that the universe contained. Encouraged by what I considered as the progress of her recovery, I accompanied a friend in the morning in several calls, one of them as far as Kensington, and did not return till dinner-time. On my return I found a degree of anxiety in every face, and was told that she had had a sort of shivering fit, and had expressed some anxiety at the length of my absence. My sister and a friend of hers, had been engaged to dine below stairs, but a message was sent to put them off, and Mary ordered that the cloth should not be laid, as usual, in the room immediately under her on the first floor, but in the ground-floor parlour. I felt a pang at having been so long and so unseasonably absent, and determined that I would not repeat the fault.

In the evening she had a second shivering fit, the symptoms of which were in the highest degree alarming. Every muscle of the body trembled, the teeth chattered, and the bed shook under her. This continued probably for five minutes. She told me, after it was over, that it had been a struggle between life and death, and that she had been more than once, in the course of it, at the point of expiring. I now apprehend these to have been the symptoms of a decided mortification, occasioned by the part of the placenta that remained in the womb. At the time however I was far from considering it in that light. When I went for Dr Poignand, between two and three o'clock on the morning of Thursday, despair was in my heart. The fact of the adhesion of the placenta was stated to me; and, ignorant as I was of obstetrical science, I felt as if the death of Mary was in a manner decided. But hope had re-visited my bosom; and her cheerings were so delightful, that I hugged her obstinately to my heart. I was only mortified at what appeared to me a new delay in the recovery I so earnestly longed for. I immediately sent for Dr Fordyce, who had been with her in the morning, as well as on the three preceding days. Dr Poignand had also called this morning, but declined paying any further visits, as we had thought proper to call in Dr Fordyce.

The progress of the disease was now uninterrupted. On Tuesday I found it necessary again to call in Dr Fordyce in the afternoon, who brought with him Dr Clarke of New Burlington-street, under the idea that some operation might be necessary. I have already said, that I pertinaciously persisted in viewing the fair side of things; and therefore the interval between Sunday and Tuesday evening, did not pass without some mixture of cheerfulness. On Monday, Dr Fordyce forbad the child's having the breast, and we therefore procured puppies to draw off the milk. This occasioned some pleasantry of Mary with me and the other attendants. Nothing could exceed the equanimity, the patience and affectionateness of the poor sufferer. I intreated her to recover; I dwelt with trembling fondness on every favourable circumstance; and, as far as it was possible in so dreadful a situation, she, by her smiles and kind speeches, rewarded my affection.

Wednesday was to me the day of greatest torture in the melancholy series. It was now decided that the only chance of supporting her through what she had to suffer, was by supplying her rather freely with wine. This task was devolved upon me. I began about four o'clock in the afternoon. But for me, totally ignorant of the nature of diseases and of the human frame, thus to play with a life that now seemed all that was dear to me in the universe, was too dreadful a task. I knew neither what was too much, nor what was too little. Having begun, I felt compelled, under every disadvantage, to go on. This lasted for three hours. Towards the end of that time, I happened foolishly to ask the servant who came out of the room, 'What she thought of her mistress?' she replied, 'that, in her judgment, she was going as fast as possible.' There are moments, when any creature that lives, has power to drive one into madness. I seemed to know the absurdity of this reply; but that was of no consequence. It added to the measure of my distraction. A little after seven I intreated a friend to go for Mr Carlisle and bring him instantly wherever he was to be found. He had voluntarily called on the patient on the preceding Saturday, and two or three times since. He had seen her that morning, and had been earnest in recommending the wine-diet. That day he dined four miles out of town, on the side of the metropolis, which was furthest from us. Notwithstanding this, my friend returned with him after three-quarters of an hour's absence. No one who knows my friend, will wonder either at his eagerness or success, when I name Mr Basil Montagu. The sight of Mr Carlisle thus unexpectedly, gave me a stronger alleviating sensation, than I thought it possible to experience.

Mr Carlisle left us no more from Wednesday evening, to the hour of her death. It was impossible to exceed his kindness and affectionate attention. It excited in every spectator a sentiment like adoration. His conduct was uniformly tender and anxious, ever upon the watch, observing every symptom, and eager to improve every favourable appearance. If skill or attention could have saved her, Mary would still live.

In addition to Mr Carlisle's constant presence, she had Dr Fordyce and Dr Clarke every day. She had for nurses, or rather for friends, watching every occasion to serve her, Mrs Fenwick, author of an excellent novel, entitled *Secrecy*, another very kind and judicious lady, and a favourite female servant. I was scarcely ever out of the room. Four friends, Mr Fenwick, Mr Basil Montagu, Mr Marshal, and Mr Dyson, sat up nearly the whole of the last week of her existence in the house, to be dispatched, on any errand, to any part of the metropolis, at a moment's warning.

Mr Carlisle being in the chamber, I retired to bed for a few hours on Wednesday night. Towards morning he came into my room with an account that the patient was surprisingly better. I went instantly into the chamber. But I now sought to suppress every idea of hope. The greatest anguish I have any conception of, consists in that crushing of a new-born hope which I had already two or three times experienced. If Mary recovered, it was well, and I should see it time enough. But it was too mighty a thought to bear being trifled with, and turned out and admitted in this abrupt way.

I had reason to rejoice in the firmness of my gloomy thoughts, when, about ten o'clock on Thursday evening, Mr Carlisle told us to prepare ourselves, for we had reason to expect the fatal event every moment. To my thinking, she did not appear to be in that state of total exhaustion, which I supposed to precede death; but it is probable that death does not always take place by that gradual process I had pictured to myself; a sudden pang may accelerate his arrival. She did not die on Thursday night.

Till now it does not appear that she had any serious thoughts of dying; but on Friday and Saturday, the two last days of her life, she occasionally spoke as if she expected it. This was however only at intervals; the thought did not seem to dwell upon her mind. Mr Carlisle rejoiced in this. He observed, and there is great force in the suggestion, that there is no more pitiable object, than a sick man, that knows he is dying. The thought must be expected to destroy his courage, to co-operate with the disease, and to counteract every favourable effort of nature.

On these two days her faculties were in too decayed a state, to be able to follow any train of ideas with force or any accuracy of connection. Her religion, as I have already shown, was not calculated to be the torment of a sick bed; and, in fact, during her whole illness, not one word of a religious cast fell from her lips.

She was affectionate and compliant to the last. I observed on Friday and Saturday nights, that, whenever her attendants recommended to her to sleep, she discovered her willingness to yield, by breathing, perhaps for the space of a minute, in the manner of a person that sleeps, though the effort, from the state of her disorder, usually proved ineffectual.

She was not tormented by useless contradiction. One night the servant, from an error in judgment teased her with idle expostulations, but she complained of it grievously, and it was corrected. 'Pray, pray, do not let her reason with me,' was her expression. Death itself is scarcely so dreadful to the enfeebled frame, as the monotonous importunity of nurses everlastingly repeated.

Seeing that every hope was extinct, I was very desirous of obtaining from her any directions, that she might wish to have followed after her decease. Accordingly, on Saturday morning, I talked to her for a good while of the two children. In conformity to Mr Carlisle's maxim of not impressing the idea of death, I was obliged to manage my expressions. I therefore affected to proceed wholly upon the ground of her having been very ill, and that it would be some time before she could expect to be well; wishing her to tell me any thing that she would choose to have done respecting the children, as they would now be principally under my care. After having repeated this idea to her in a great variety of forms, she at length said, with a significant tone of voice, 'I know what you are thinking of,' but added, that she had nothing to communicate to me upon the subject.

The shivering fits had ceased entirely for the two last days. Mr Carlisle observed that her continuance was almost miraculous, and he was on the watch for favourable appearances, believing it highly improper to give up all hope, and remarking, that perhaps one in a million, of persons in her state might possibly recover. I conceive that not one in a million, unites so good a constitution of body and of mind.

These were the amusements of persons in the very gulph of despair. At six o'clock on Sunday morning, September the tenth, Mr Carlisle called me from my bed to which I had retired at one, in conformity to my request, that I might not be left to receive all at once the intelligence that she was no more. She expired at twenty minutes before eight.

Her remains were deposited, on the fifteenth of September, at ten o'clock in the morning, in the church-yard of the parish church of St Pancras, Middlesex. A few of the persons she most esteemed, attended the ceremony; and a plain monument is now erecting on the spot, by some of her friends, with the following inscription:

MARY WOLLSTONECRAFT GODWIN,
Author of
A VINDICATION
OF THE RIGHTS OF WOMAN:
Born 27 April, 1759:
Died 10 September, 1797.

The loss of the world in this admirable woman, I leave to other men to collect; my own I well know, nor can it be improper to describe it. I do not here allude to the personal pleasures I enjoyed in her conversation: these increased every day, in proportion as we knew each other better, and as our mutual confidence increased. They can be measured only by the treasures of her mind, and the virtues of her heart. But this is a subject for meditation, not for words. What I purposed alluding to, was the improvement that I have for ever lost.

We had cultivated our powers (if I may venture to use this sort of language) in different directions; I chiefly an attempt at logical and metaphysical distinction, she a taste for the picturesque. One of the leading passions of my mind has been an anxious desire not to be deceived. This has led me to view the topics of my reflection on all sides; and to examine and re-examine without end, the questions that interest me.

But it was not merely (to judge at least from all the reports of my memory in this respect) the difference of propensities, that made the difference in our intellectual habits. I have been stimulated, as long as I can remember, by an ambition for intellectual distinction; but, as long as I can remember, I have been discouraged, when I have endeavoured to cast the sum of my intellectual value, by finding that I did not possess, in the degree of some other men, an intuitive perception of intellectual beauty. I have perhaps a strong and lively sense of the pleasures of the imagination; but I have seldom been right in assigning to them their proportionate value, but by dint of persevering examination, and the change and correction of my first opinions.

What I wanted in this respect, Mary possessed, in a degree superior to any other person I ever knew. The strength of her mind lay in intuition. She was often right, by this means only, in matters of mere speculation. Her religion, her philosophy, (in both of which the errors were comparatively few, and the strain dignified and generous) were, as I have already said, the pure result of feeling and taste. She adopted one opinion, and rejected another, spontaneously, by a sort of tact, and the force of a cultivated imagination; and yet, though perhaps, in the strict sense of the term, she reasoned little, it is surprising what a degree of soundness is to be found in her determinations. But, if this quality was of use to her in topics that seem the proper province of reasoning, it was much more so in matters directly appealing to the intellectual taste. In a robust and unwavering judgment of this sort, there is a kind of witchcraft; when it decides justly, it produces a responsive vibration in every ingenuous mind. In this sense, my oscillation and scepticism were fixed by her boldness. When a true opinion emanated in this way from another mind, the conviction produced in my own assumed a similar character, instantaneous and firm. This species of intellect probably differs from the other, chiefly in the relation of earlier and later. What the one perceives instantaneously (circumstances having produced in it, either a premature attention to objects of this sort, or a greater boldness of decision) the other receives only by degrees. What it wants, seems to be nothing more than a minute attention to first impressions, and a just appreciation of them; habits that are never so effectually generated, as by the daily recurrence of a striking example.

This light was lent to me for a very short period, and is now extinguished for ever!

While I have described the improvement I was in the act of receiving, I believe I have put down the leading traits of her intellectual character.

APPENDIX

Three Passages rewritten for the Second Edition

1. From Chapter Six, concerning Henry Fuseli

The delight she enjoyed in his society, she transferred by association to his person. To understand this, we have only to recollect how dear to persons of sensibility is the exercise of the affections. A sound morality requires that 'nothing human should be regarded by us with indifference;' but it is impossible that we should not feel the strongest interest for those persons, whom we know most intimately, and whose welfare and sympathies are united to our own. True wisdom will recommend to us individual attachments; for with them our minds are more thoroughly maintained in activity and life than they can be under the privation of them, and it is better that man should be a living being, than a stock or a stone. True virtue will sanction this recommendation, since it is the object of virtue to produce happiness, and since the man who lives in the midst of domestic relations, will have many opportunities of conferring pleasure, minute in the detail, yet not trivial in the amount, without interfering with the purposes of general benevolence. Nay, by kindling his sensibility, and harmonizing his soul, they may be expected, if he is endowed with a liberal and manly spirit, to render him more prompt in the service of strangers and of the public.

But, in the catalogue of domestic charities, there are none so capable of affording strong and permanent delight, as that of two persons of opposite sexes who have conceived a preference for each other. Human beings differ so much in their tempers and views, that, except in cases of a tender attachment, cohabitation brings with it small prospect of harmony and happiness. The connection between parents and children, between grown persons and young, is of too unequal a nature; and is bounded and restrained by a sense of responsibility on the one side, and the inattention and heedlessness particularly incident to the other. The charm of domestic life consists in a mutual desire to study each other's gratification; and this can scarcely subsist in sufficient force, but in this particular connection.

Mary had now lived for upwards of thirty years in a state of celibacy and seclusion. As her sensibilities were exquisitely acute, she had felt this sort of banishment from social charities, so frequent in a state of high civilization and refinement, more painfully than persons in general are likely to feel it. Or rather, as I believe, she suffered occasional accesses of uneasiness, torpor, and vacuity, without having clearly traced the sources and remedy of the evil. She was like what we are told of those lofty and aspiring geniuses, who, being formed for busy scenes and daring projects, find the activity of their temper, when debarred its proper field, corroding and preying upon itself. The sentiments which Mr Fuseli excited in her mind, taught her the secret; to which she was so long in a manner a stranger.

Let it not however be imagined, that this was any other than the dictate of a most refined sentiment, and the simple deduction of morality and reason. Never was there a woman on the face of the earth more alien to that mire and grossness, in which the sensual part of our species are delighted to wallow. Superior at the same time to the idleness of romance, and the pretence of an ideal philosophy, no one knew more perfectly how to assign to the enjoyments of affection their respective rank, or to maintain in virgin and unsullied purity the chasteness of her mind.

It happened in the present case that Mr Fuseli was already married; and, in visiting at his house, his wife became the acquaintance of Mary. Mary did not disguise from herself how desirable it would have been, that the man in whom she discovered qualities calling forth all the strength of her attachment, should have been equally free with herself. But she chearfully submitted to the empire of circumstances. She conceived it practicable to cultivate a distinguishing affection, and to foster it by the endearments of personal intercourse and reciprocation of kindness, without departing from the consideration due to his previous engagements. She scorned to suppose, that she could feel a struggle, in conforming to the laws she should lay down to her conduct.

2. From Chapter Eight, concerning Wollstonecraft's suicide attempt

It was night when she arrived at Putney, and by that time it had begun to rain with great violence. The rain suggested to her the idea of walking up and down the bridge, till her clothes were thoroughly drenched and heavy with the wet, which she did for half an hour without meeting a human being. She then leaped from the top of the bridge, but still seemed to find a difficulty in sinking, which she endeavoured to counteract by pressing her clothes closely round her. After some time she became insensible; but she always spoke of the pain she underwent as such, that, though she could afterwards have determined upon almost any other species of voluntary death, it would have been impossible for her to resolve upon encountering the same sensations again. I am doubtful, whether this is to be ascribed to the mere nature of suffocation, or was not rather owing to the preternatural action of a desperate spirit. *Second edition adds:* How strange is the condition of our nature! The whole scene of human life may at last be pronounced a delusion! Speculation for ever deceives us, and is the appropriate office of castle-builders; but the active concerns of life cheat us still more! Mary was in the first instance mistaken in the object of her attachment, imputing to him qualities which, in the trial, proved to be imaginary. By insensible degrees she proceeded to stake her life upon the consequences of her error: and, for the disappointment of this choice, for a consideration so foreign to the true end of her powers

and cultivation, she was willing to consign those powers and that cultivation, pregnant as they were with pleasure to herself and gratification
to others, formed to adorn society, and give a relish the most delicate
and unrivalled to domestic life, as well as, through the medium of the
press, to delight, instruct, and reform mankind – she was willing, I
say, to consign all these to premature destruction! How often is the
sagacity of our moral judgment reserved for the hour of meditation,
and how little does it sometimes bestead us in the time of our greatest
need!

3. *From Chapter Ten, summarizing Wollstonecraft's 'intellectual character'*

A circumstance by which the two sexes are particularly distinguished
from each other, is, that the one is accustomed more to the exercise
of its reasoning powers, and the other of its feelings. Women have a
frame of body more delicate and susceptible of impression than men,
and, in proportion as they receive a less intellectual education, are more
unreservedly under the empire of feeling. Feeling is liable to become
a source of erroneous decisions, because a mind not accustomed to
logical analysis, cannot be expected accurately to discriminate between
the simple dictates of an ingenuous mind, and the factitious sentiments
of a partial education. Habits of deduction enable us to correct this
defect. But habits of deduction may generate habits of sophistry; and
scepticism and discussion, while they undermine our prejudices, have
sometimes a tendency to weaken or distort our feelings. Hence we may
infer one of the advantages accruing from the association of persons
of an opposite sex: they may be expected to counteract the principal
mistake into which either is in danger to fall.

Mary and myself perhaps each carried farther than to its common
extent the characteristic of the sexes to which we belonged. I have
been stimulated, as long as I can remember, by the love of intellectual
distinction; but, as long as I can remember, I have been discouraged,

when casting the sum of my intellectual value, by finding that I did not possess, in the degree of some other persons, an intuitive sense of the pleasures of the imagination. Perhaps I feel them as vividly as most men; but it is often rather by an attentive consideration, than an instantaneous survey. They have been liable to fail of their effect in the first experiment; and my scepticism has often led me anxiously to call in the approved decisions of taste, as a guide to my judgment, or a countenance to my enthusiasm. One of the leading passions of my mind has been an anxious desire not to be deceived. This has led me to view the topics of my reflection on all sides, and to examine and re-examine without end the questions that interest me. Endless disquisition however is not always the parent of certainty.

What I wanted in this respect, Mary possessed in a degree superior to any other person I ever knew. Her feelings had a character of peculiar strength and decision; and the discovery of them, whether in matters of taste or of moral virtue, she found herself unable to control. She had viewed the objects of nature with a lively sense and an ardent admiration, and had developed their beauties. Her education had been fortunately free from the prejudices of system and bigotry, and her sensitive and generous spirit was left to the spontaneous exercise of its own decisions. The warmth of her heart defended her from artificial rules of judgment; and it is therefore surprising what a degree of soundness pervaded her sentiments. In the strict sense of the term, she had reasoned comparatively little; and she was therefore little subject to diffidence and scepticism. Yet a mind more candid in perceiving and retracting error, when it was pointed out to her, perhaps never existed. This arose naturally out of the directness of her sentiments, and her fearless and unstudied veracity.

A companion like this, excites and animates the mind. From such an one we imbibe, what perhaps I principally wanted, the habit of minutely attending to first impressions, and justly appreciating them. Her taste awakened mine; her sensibility determined me to a careful development of my feelings. She delighted to open her heart to the beauties of nature; and her propensity in this respect led me to a more intimate contemplation of them. My scepticism in judging, yielded to the coincidence of another's judgment; and especially when the judgment of that other was such, that the more I made experiment of it, the more was I convinced of its rectitude.

The improvement I had reason to promise myself, was however yet in its commencement, when a fatal event, hostile to the moral interests of mankind, ravished from me the light of my steps, and left to me nothing but the consciousness of what I had possessed, and must now possess no more!

While I have described the improvement I was in the act of receiving, I believe I have put down the leading traits of her intellectual character from which it flowed.

FURTHER READING

Mary Wollstonecraft: *A Vindication of the Rights of Woman*, (1792), edited by Miriam Brody Kramnick, Penguin, 1982

——*A Short Residence in Sweden* (1796) and William Godwin, *Memoirs* (1798) edited by Richard Holmes, Penguin Classics, 1987

William Godwin: *St Leon*, (novel, with Preface describing Mary), 1799

Thomas Brown MD: *The Wanderer in Norway*, (poem) 1816

William Hazlitt: 'Mr Godwin' in *The Spirit of the Age*, 1825

Anne Elwood: *Memoirs of the Literary Ladies of England*, 1842

Charles Kegan Paul: *William Godwin: His Friends and Contemporaries*, 2 vols., 1876

Elizabeth Robins Pennell: *Mary Wollstonecraft Godwin*, Eminent Women Series, 1885

Millicent Garret Fawcett: 'Introduction' to *A Vindication of the Rights of Woman*, Centenary edition, 1892

Virginia Woolf: 'Mary Wollstonecraft' in *the Common Reader*, Second Series, 1932

Ralph M. Wardle: *Mary Wollstonecraft: A Critical Biography*, 1952

Claire Tomalin: *The Life and Death of Mary Wollstonecraft*, 1974, Penguin 1992

Don Locke: *A Fantasy of Reason: the Life and Thought of William Godwin*, Routledge, 1980

William St Clair: *The Godwins and the Shelleys: the Biography of a Family*, Faber, 1989

Clarissa Campbell Orr: *Wollstonecraft's Daughters: Womanhood in England and France, 1780–1920*, Manchester University Press, 1996

Janet Todd: *Mary Wollstonecraft: A Revolutionary Life*, Weidenfeld and Nicolson, 2000

Cora Kaplin: 'Mary Wollstonecraft's Reception and Legacy', in *The Cambridge Companion to Mary Wollstonecraft*, Cambridge University Press, 2002

——*The Collected Letters of Mary Wollstonecraft*, edited by Janet Todd, Allen Lane, 2003

Barbara Taylor: *Mary Wollstonecraft and the Feminist Imagination*, Cambridge University Press, 2003

Lyndall Gordon: *Mary Wollstonecraft: A New Genus*, Little Brown, 2004

INDEX

INDEX